WEB OF BETRAYAL

WEB OF BETRAYAL

MURDER IN IRELAND'S BRUTAL GANGLAND

NICOLA TALLANT

First published in the UK by Eriu
An imprint of Black & White Publishing Group
A Bonnier Books UK company

4th Floor, Victoria House,
Bloomsbury Square,
London, WC1B 4DA

Owned by Bonnier Books
Sveavägen 56, Stockholm, Sweden

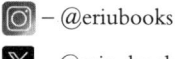 – @eriubooks

– @eriu_books

Trade Paperback – 978-1-80418-537-7
Ebook – 978-1-80418-715-9
Audio – 978-1-80418-784-5

All rights reserved. No part of the publication may be reproduced, stored in a retrieval system, transmitted or circulated in any form or by any means, electronic, mechanical, photocopying, recording or otherwise, without prior permission in writing of the publisher.

A CIP catalogue of this book is available from the British Library.

Typeset by IDSUK (Data Connection) Ltd
Printed and bound by Clays Ltd, Elcograf S.p.A

1 3 5 7 9 10 8 6 4 2

Copyright © Nicola Tallant 2024

Nicola Tallant has asserted their moral right to be identified as the author of this Work in accordance with the Copyright, Designs and Patents Act 1988.

Every reasonable effort has been made to trace copyright holders of material reproduced in this book, but if any have been inadvertently overlooked the publishers would be glad to hear from them.

Eriu is an imprint of Bonnier Books UK
www.bonnierbooks.co.uk

Then one of the Twelve – the one called Judas Iscariot – went to the chief priests and asked, 'What are you willing to give me if I deliver him over to you?' So they counted out for him thirty pieces of silver. From then on, Judas watched for an opportunity to hand him over"

Matthew 26:14

Contents

Prologue		ix
Chapter 1	A New Order	1
Chapter 2	A Killing Boom	31
Chapter 3	An Opportunity to Kill	73
Chapter 4	A Murder and a Town at War	101
Chapter 5	The Jury has Decided	121
Chapter 6	The Gym Bag	141
Chapter 7	The Torso	165
Chapter 8	The Murder of a Killer	181
Chapter 9	A Romance and a Double-Cross	195
Chapter 10	The Case against the Alleged Killers	215
Chapter 11	'It's a very, very, very good theory, your honour'	225
Chapter 12	The Sligo Connection	243
Chapter 13	Untangling the Web	255

Prologue

I'd never got out of Dublin so quickly. I had to be careful not to drive too fast as I knew there were police everywhere. With nine points on my licence I couldn't afford another speeding ticket or I'd be off the road. I'd hung the press pass journalists had been issued as essential workers from the rear view mirror so I could be waved on at any checkpoint I met, but I needn't have worried: when I was flagged down just outside Drogheda the police officer looked into the car, smiled, and said, 'Well, I can guess where you're off to.'

It was 4 April 2020 and the body of Robbie Lawlor was still lying in the front garden of a red-brick terraced house in Ardoyne, a Republican stronghold in north Belfast. Just before midday he'd arrived there in a car and called to the door but instead of being let in a gunman had run at him and pumped him full of bullets. Three members of Limerick's notorious Dundon gang had been arrested and from what I could gather they had been with Lawlor when he was shot and had likely driven him into Ardoyne. A criminal from Belfast was being named as the one who'd lured him to his death and another with strong dissident links was about to be arrested. As for who had orchestrated the hit ... Who wanted Lawlor dead? Well, that was a case of take your pick. The last chaotic four months of Lawlor's crazed existence had pitted him against an array of some of the most dangerous and vicious criminals in the country. Lawlor had been a dead man walking long before the first familiar crack of gunshots had cut through the morning quiet in Ardoyne. If ever there was proof that gangland was in disarray and that criminals didn't obey Covid travel bans, this was it.

My phone hopped the whole way north, dying only as I crossed the border at Newry in a kind of a communications no man's land before springing back to life a few kilometres later. It was a Saturday and I was on a deadline to file what would no doubt be a front page splash for the *Sunday World*. After all, it wasn't every day that a criminal of Robbie Lawlor's reputation was taken out in broad daylight on a residential street where drug dealers from Dublin once feared to venture.

In Belfast I first met with a photographer at the Ardoyne Community Centre, where we abandoned my car and, in total disregard of our Covid working guidelines, jumped into his Jeep. I'd been around Ardoyne before but I'd never paid it much notice. This time it struck me how linear it was: rows and rows of identical terraced houses and giant murals commemorating the Easter Rising of 1916 and those who'd been killed in the Troubles and the Famine. Green, white and orange, the colours of the Irish flag, seemed to be spray-painted everywhere, with messages about 'saluting the men and women of violence' and supporting the IRA. Tricolours hung outside houses and graffiti reminded those who hadn't spotted the clues that they were in nationalist Belfast. Just two hours of motorway separates Belfast from Dublin, where I grew up, yet the murals of Ardoyne tell a tale of two vastly different cities, one where a war raged over decades and the other that knew peace and looked the other way.

'Will we go straight to Etna Drive and then meet yer man?' the photographer asked me loudly, pulling me from my thoughts. 'Yer man' was an underworld contact who'd agreed to meet me to impart what he'd heard about the murder of Lawlor and the involvement of dissident IRA figures. He was himself a known dangerous criminal who mixed in the melting pot of paramilitaries, drug dealers and extortionists who made up Belfast's strange and dangerous underworld. He was also a Covid denier who believed in chemtrails and aliens. 'Yes, let's do the scene first,' I said.

At Etna Drive men in white suits with cameras and laboratory bottles swarmed inside the tiny terraced home where a gunman had run at Lawlor as he walked towards the front door. A white tent stood in the front garden, covering his body until officers from the Police Service of Northern Ireland (PSNI) deemed it time to move it to a morgue for a post-mortem. I looked around for any neighbours who might have seen what had happened. One man told me the victim had been brandishing a gun but then he'd been shot three times and that a car had sped away. 'Was he really a Dublin drug dealer?' a woman asked me incredulously. 'Like, what was he *doing* here in Ardoyne?' Nobody knew immediately who Lawlor was; his name simply wasn't an eyebrow-raiser as it was in the South. But everyone had heard the story of his most recent victim, the teenage boy Keane Mulready-Woods, who'd been kidnapped, tortured and dismembered. His legs had been left in a holdall near the stronghold of a rival drug boss known as 'Mr Big' and his head in a car boot initially destined for the compound of violent mobster Cornelius Price before the mission was abandoned. That sequence of events was just about as narco style as Ireland had ever seen and had set Robbie Lawlor apart even in the violent world he inhabited.

'Yer man' met us in the driveway of a very peculiar property outside Belfast. It had been added to many times since it had been built, and the extensions seemed like square boxes, giving the impression of a Lego construction. It sat on top of a hill and might perhaps have once been a nursing home or a bed and breakfast. There were so many rooms and no flow to it. After some pleasantries I found myself standing with him on a raised flower bed looking at the sky. 'Do you see them, Nicola? Do you?' he asked, pointing upwards. 'I do of course,' I said. 'That's toxins. They are coming out of the planes. The government put them in,' he informed me. I thought of pointing out that Northern Ireland, at that time, had no government due to a political scandal around a renewable energy scheme, but thought better of it. 'I see. I really do see it. But tell me about Robbie Lawlor. What have you heard?' I hoped my sudden change of topic from chemtrails to murder wouldn't unbalance our finely tuned conversation, but 'Yer man' seemed happy enough to divulge what he knew. Lawlor was trying to muscle in on some drug territories in the North, he said, and was put in his box by the locals. The story rambled on about revenge and debts and about how his death would be a message to all 'your guys' to stay south of the border – by 'your guys' he meant drug dealers from the Republic of Ireland. I thanked 'yer man', promised to drop in to see him when next in the North, graciously took some literature on bad governments poisoning our minds and headed off to consider what I knew.

It was a strange one. There was something very murky about what had happened that morning in Ardoyne. In the custody of the PSNI were Ger Dundon and his nephew Levi Killeen, the son of the notorious John Dundon who along with his brother Wayne had rained terror on the south-western city of Limerick over a decade of bloodshed, along with another associate with the unusual name of Quincy Bramble. They'd been lifted near the scene of the murder in a Volvo car. I knew that Dundon and Lawlor had been friends; they'd met in prison – but what did that count for in the underworld, where loyalty is only skin-deep? It was difficult to imagine that Lawlor had attempted to carry out a gun attack in such unfamiliar territory as Ardoyne and that the tables had been turned on him, but he had been so unpredictable in the preceding months that anything was possible. And if this was a planned hit on Lawlor it seemed a strange place to target him. After all, there were plenty of opportunities down south where his enemies knew their territory and escape routes.

Lawlor had always been a wild card, but in the last few months of his life he'd become completely crazed and unpredictable. There was the terrifying violence that had cemented his reputation as gangland's most wanted man, but there were also intriguing rumours about the blonde legal professional – wealthy, well known and at the very top of her game – who seemed to have fallen for him. There was a string of gangland hits, but they paled into insignificance beside the gruesome murder of the teenager Keane Mulready-Woods. Just 17, Keane had been reported missing by his mother, Elizabeth, in Drogheda, a town in the grip of a horrendous gang feud. A day later, his legs had been discovered in a holdall dumped in a Dublin housing estate. His head was later found in the boot of a burning car. The feud was vicious and the gangs had threatened the very rule of law in the busy and prosperous commuter town. On one side was Traveller mob boss Owen Maguire and his close associate Cornelius Price. On the other were two ambitious brothers along with a volatile young thug called Paul Crosby who had attempted to stage a coup against their former bosses. And that is where Lawlor had come in on the coattails of his brother-in-law, the veteran criminal Richie Carberry, who'd backed the young guns, supplying them with drugs and guns as they fought street battles to win turf and shut down the old order. Arson attacks and assaults had intensified, culminating in the shooting of Maguire at his home on Cement Road in the summer of 2018. Maguire had survived the attack but would be confined to a wheelchair for the rest of his life. He was now in a fight to the death with the hitman, Lawlor. But the Price–Maguire faction were not the only ones who wanted Lawlor dead. He'd made lots of enemies along the way. Months before he brandished a gun at the cowering Maguire, Lawlor had shot dead Kenneth Finn, a hitman and close friend of the powerful criminal known as Mr Big who had systematically become the biggest player in the lucrative drug turf of Coolock in Dublin but who'd spread his influence across the country and into Northern Ireland.

The arrest of Dundon, Killeen and Bramble as they tried to leave Belfast that day threw up another cast of characters. Limerick's McCarthy–Dundon mob had been dismantled a decade before when Wayne and John joined their brother Dessie in jail, all serving life sentences, and the word from the prisons was that they were a spent force. But the Dundons were notorious for one thing, and that was a double-cross. As I pondered the many mobs that were immediately lining up to take their place in the story of the murder of Robbie Lawlor, I had no idea just what a complex web of betrayal had been spun. I also had no idea that days before Lawlor was shot dead, police forces across Europe had begun secretly eavesdropping on thousands of phones of those involved in organised crime. The EncroChat hack would change the understanding of the business of crime and how it worked, while the death of Lawlor and the events that would follow it would ultimately paint a detailed picture of an underworld far more ferocious and complex than most could ever imagine.

CHAPTER ONE

A New Order

They were once known as the breadbasket of Dublin, the sprawling farmlands that surrounded the city and where potatoes, vegetables and fruit were grown and transported to feed both rich and poor. Fields where cattle had once grazed became building sites as the population of the capital continued to expand throughout the 20th century and measures to move families out of dangerous tenement homes intensified. Large-scale construction of social housing in Dublin had been under way since the 1920s, first when large flat developments sprung up in the city, later in neighbourhoods like Cabra and Crumlin. But a massive wave of sprawling suburban housing estates, built both north and south of the city throughout the 1960s and 1970s, would lay the foundations of problems to come. Villages like Finglas, Coolock and Tallaght started to disappear under the weight of development. Ballymun, built in a blaze of glory as a futuristic new way of life, would become Ireland's biggest state housing disaster less than twenty years after it rose from the ground in seven towers, each 15 storeys high. The collapse of a number of city centre tenements, resulting in the deaths of elderly residents and children, had forced planners to act quickly to rehouse families, but not enough thought had gone into what would replace them.

The phased inner-city slum clearance had continued into the early 1980s, at which point council houses with a Coolock address, like Darndale, Donaghmede, Kilbarrack, Edenmore, Moatview and Belcamp, made up the largest stock of bricks and mortar owned by the State. By then the image and reputation of Coolock and nearby Ballymun were firmly embedded in the nation's psyche as crime blackspots. As in other areas of the capital, the planners had had the ambition to create a new way of life for new communities with lots of green open spaces and fresh opportunities for families. But the reality was rather different. By the time the final houses were being built, Coolock, with a population of over 20,000, had a reputation of being dangerous, dilapidated, neglected and a centre of poverty, crime, violence, drug use and dealing. The location of two permanent Traveller halting sites, the largest in the country, side by side with the impoverished social housing schemes would also be questioned in the future as less than ideal planning.

Unemployment lay at the heart of the problem in the 1980s. In 1981, according to the Economic and Social Research Institute (ESRI), there were 125,700 people out of work nationally. In 1986, by which time the recession had firmly taken hold, that figure had risen to 227,500. Coolock was hit harder than many other parts of the country and the unemployment rate stood officially at over 27 per cent, about 8 per cent per cent higher than the national average. But the problem was much worse in reality. One study carried out by Bonnybrook unemployment agency put the figures even higher, at 45–65 per cent unemployment. When a 14-hour concert, Self Aid, took place in the RDS, Dublin in 1986, to highlight the unemployment problem in Ireland, a quarter of a million people were out of work.

The fire that engulfed the Stardust nightclub in the early hours of 14 February 1981 had also had long-reaching effects on the local community. More than 840 people had attended the disco and 48 had died, while another 214 were injured. The communities of Artane and Coolock, home to most of the young clubbers, embarked on decades of legal wrangling, political rows and huge personal traumas as they tried to navigate the overwhelming tragedy in their fight for the truth. By the end of the 1980s Roddy Doyle's novel *The Commitments*, set in the fictitious Barrytown, would put Coolock on the big screen in a movie directed by Alan Parker. Urban horses, bought in city markets, thundering through littered fields and ridden bareback by young cowboys through concrete jungles may have been an unfamiliar sight to those who watched the film, but to those who lived in Coolock and nearby Ballymun they were part of the landscape. Support groups, youth projects, parenting help centres and unemployment offices were opened to help the depression, but among the many reasons that the migration of families from the inner city to the new suburbs hadn't gone as planned was that the schemes had failed to provide infrastructure, community or diversity. Dublin's population profile had changed over those thirty years of building in Coolock, with more young people than in previous decades, intensifying the entrenched unemployment problem that would last most of the next decade.

At the same time heroin had begun to take hold of Dublin. It showed up first in the north and south inner city in the late 1970s, a time when traditional industries like dock work were faltering and a sense of hopelessness had started to seep in. It quickly got a hold on an impoverished, alienated generation and spread its tentacles outwards. By the 1980s social housing estates across Dublin were in the grip of the epidemic, with communities fighting a losing battle against the drug. Activists took to the streets under the umbrella movement Concerned Parents Against Drugs and ran many dealers out of their homes, but heroin was more powerful than anyone could imagine, and despite their efforts it wiped out a generation of users, scarring their families for ever. Ballymun was one of the worst-hit areas and it was in the stairwells of its flats that dealers, often from surrounding suburbs, peddled their product. Needles lay everywhere, addicts slept where they fell and the stench of urine seeped into the concrete blocks as horses wandered the wastelands.

A study conducted in the early 1980s, the Bradshaw Report, focused on the north inner city and found an overwhelming prevalence of young people under the age of 24 taking the drug intravenously. The report sparked the establishment of the first Government Task Force on Drug Abuse. Leaning heavily on a legal route to help the problem, it resulted in the Misuse of Drugs Act 1984 which laid out harsher penalties for those possessing and selling drugs. By the mid-1980s AIDS added to the crisis, with intravenous drug users being in the highest risk category. Methadone maintenance programmes were introduced and policy-makers advised that needle exchanges could help lower the risk of infection. But the government was slow to act, and gardaí were not equipped to deal with the rise of drug use and sale in heavily populated estates or with the resulting crime that went with it. While the communities did try to fight back, ten years into the crisis many had grown tired of the unwinnable battle. Many clamoured to get out and move their families to areas seen as more prosperous. Others were forced to stay and watch their children grow up surrounded by massive open-air drug supermarkets familiar to addicts and dealers, painfully aware of how their areas were being labelled.

In his report *Darndale: A Long View of an Enduring Challenge – A Socio-economic & Community Plan*, carried out for Dublin City Council in 2020, former Assistant Commissioner Dr Jack Nolan described the reputation of Darndale at the time:

> As far back as 1991, graffiti at the entrance to Darndale announced 'Welcome to Darndale – twinned with Beirut', this was at a time when the civil war in Lebanon was coming to an end and Beirut had been largely destroyed by the conflict. While this was undoubtedly an exercise in mischief and black humour, it nevertheless was indicative of some elements of the local population's opinion, image and self worth of the area.

The former top garda also pointed to a so-called 'Surrender Grant' scheme introduced by Dublin City Council as hurrying the decline. It offered a grant of up to £10,000 to local authority tenants to leave their homes, buy in the private sector and make way for new council residents. A report on the scheme from 1987 showed that 75 per cent of applicants were concentrated in three housing areas, including Darndale. The Threshold housing charity studied the consequences of the scheme and warned that it would continue to have lasting and dire effects on the area:

> The grant undoubtedly enabled people who might not otherwise have been able to do so to purchase a house in the private sector. Their exodus, however, had serious consequences in these areas of high take-up of the grant. Already existing problems were heightened and further ones created. Communities where unemployment was already high suffered the loss of many of those people who had jobs. Income levels dropped and services in the areas deteriorated. Many of the vacant houses were vandalised. The community was substantially deprived of its leaders as they were the ones to move out with the grant.

The report went on to say that the people who moved out were replaced with other marginalised groups like lone parents and homeless single men.

As the country faced into the 1990s, a period that would see massive social change and financial opportunities for many, a second wave of heroin was about to hit the already beleaguered communities. While cannabis was enjoying its golden era, heroin was making a comeback, sweeping through underprivileged communities once more, this time to mop up another generation of hopeless addicts. Controlled by George 'The Penguin' Mitchell and his many henchmen, including Michael 'Roly' Cronin, Thomas 'The Boxer' Mullen and Derek 'Maradona' Dunne, the drug found a fresh crop of customers in exactly the same inner-city and social housing sprawls of north and south Dublin as it had before. The new users were young, just like those who had been wiped out by the first epidemic of the 1980s, but they were convinced that by smoking it and not injecting they could survive overdosing and the worst ravages of its long-term effects.

By 1993 Independent TD Tony Gregory was so concerned at the level of heroin back on the streets that he asked the then Minister for Justice Máire Geoghegan-Quinn if she had a plan to crack down on its open sale on the streets.

> Will the Minister accept that there must be something seriously wrong when she was told in February last by the Garda authorities there was no evidence to suggest any significant increase in the supply of heroin while the reality is that in 1992 the highest amount of heroin was seized since 1986 and heroin and other drugs are openly on sale in this city? Does the Minister accept that whole areas of this city are being subjected to intimidation by street gangs pushing drugs, the drug treatment centres in those areas are being swamped by new addicts and that the problem is getting out of control?

Gregory went on to suggest that a lack of Garda resources coupled with an out-of-touch judiciary meant that drug dealers were free to operate as they pleased, but Geoghegan-Quinn rejected the suggestions, saying that the matter was of the highest importance and that the Gardaí were fully resourced.

On the streets there was also a new kid in town that was giving drugs a fresh, cool image. The rise of ecstasy and the dance culture that surrounded it created a whole new customer base for hungry customers who would likely never have taken opioids. 'E' made drug-taking both recreational and acceptable for a diverse social grouping known as ravers. In clubs like The Asylum crowds of middle- and working-class socialites gathered to dance the night away with music chosen by celebrity DJs. By the summer of 1994 it was clear that the competition was ferocious when it came to the money involved in the sale of ecstasy when a teenager was shot in the stomach during an argument between rival gangs outside the club. While the vibes around ecstasy were all about love, the suppliers feeding the market were violent and ruthless. When dealer Mark Dwyer fell out with his friend's father over a missing stash of ecstasy tablets he was tortured to death after being abducted from his Dublin flat. To cover his tracks the notorious killer 'Cotton Eye' Joe Delaney beat and then shot Dwyer before savagely beating up his own son Scott and leaving him with the body to throw detectives off the scent. Scott Delaney, who now goes by Scott Knight, would later tell a YouTube channel that in the early 1990s he lived like Pablo Escobar, selling 30,000 ecstasy tablets a week.

Cocaine too was creeping into the drugs market and it wouldn't take long for the entrepreneurial dealers, young and old, to see its potential beyond the richer classes in society. While a growing youth population who had been left behind by progress saw career opportunities in the new and growing drug market, a wave of skilled and educated workers had more money in their pockets. The national unemployment rate fell in 1990 from 17.1 per cent to 12.9 per cent, briefly rising again in 1993 to 15.7 per cent before falling every year thereafter. In his paper *When Unemployment Disappears: Ireland in the 1990s*, Brendan Walsh of the Department of Economics at UCD laid out the transformation of the Irish labour market:

> In the 1980s Ireland's labour market was one of the worst performing in Europe. The unemployment rate rose from 7 per cent in 1979 to 17 per cent in 1986, when two thirds of the unemployed had been out of work for six months or more, almost half for over a year . . . The picture was transformed during the 1990s. The labour market situation improved, slowly at first but then at a pace that took commentators by surprise. By 2000 the unemployment rate had fallen below 4 per cent, long-term unemployment had virtually disappeared, the labour force participation rates had risen to the European average and the age-old Irish problems of emigration and population decline had given way to the highest rate of net immigration and fastest growing population in the EU.

What was labelled the 'employment miracle' in the US and hailed as a blueprint for countries in the eurozone was set to turn the 1990s into a gold rush for those involved in organised crime and the ambitious underlings who did their bidding.

As the country got richer a massive recreational drug market began to develop. There were richer pickings for those involved in crime, and as the market grew, so too did opportunities for the ambitious. The brat pack who would mark out the new gangland had grown up in the shadow of the first big-league criminals, who had become media celebrities as they muscled their way in on a crime scene long dominated by terrorism. The forefathers and mentors of the millennials were undoubtedly colourful characters. Many of them had grown up in the tenements that the new sprawls like Coolock and Ballymun replaced. They were hard men, reared poor and with a hatred of the State and all its systems. As children they'd been sent to institutions like Daingean reformatory for crimes like stealing a loaf of bread and where a later commission into child abuse would find they'd been flogged and starved and raped. The likes of Martin 'The General' Cahill had emerged from a slum at Hollyfield Buildings along with 11 siblings and had grown up to rob stately homes, carry out daring jewel heists and run rings around the Gardaí in Mickey Mouse boxer shorts. His childhood had undoubtedly been carved out by poverty and an alcoholic father who regularly spent the family wage on drink. The children, including the notorious Martin, began to steal out of necessity to feed their siblings and moved in and out of institutions between robbing houses in far more affluent neighbourhoods. The General once claimed that Daingean was his primary school, St Patrick's Institution his secondary school and Mountjoy Prison his university. 'They taught me everything I know,' he said. He made a mockery of the Gardaí throughout his career with his scams and his robberies. He died staring down the barrel of a gun, but his legend was cemented when director John Boorman made a movie about him starring Brendan Gleeson as the crime boss.

Cahill's sidekick Martin 'The Viper' Foley survived kidnaps, repeated assassination attempts, grinned for the cameras with his trademark handlebar moustache and regularly did interviews with journalists, heavily disguised. He was a member of the General's inner circle and was totally loyal to him; he was also a fitness fanatic and bodybuilder who worked on his reputation as a hard man and forged close links with the Irish National Liberation Army (INLA) terrorist group and its notorious Chief of Staff Dominic 'Mad Dog' McGlinchey. The Viper was an anarchist and regularly took part in attacks on the institutions of the State, including a campaign against prison officers by a group calling themselves the Prisoners' Revenge Group and another group self-styled the Concerned Criminals Action Committee, who attempted to face down the Concerned Parents Against Drugs group.

Gerry 'The Monk' Hutch earned his reputation for being clever and wily. Born in the early 1960s, he was the youngest of a family of eight from the north inner city. He began his criminal career as the leader of a street gang known as the Bugsy Malones, who gained a fearsome reputation in the media. While the group regularly featured on the front pages as an organised grouping, their crimes were largely focused on handbag thefts, car break-ins and disorganised larceny. Hutch, like Cahill, spent stints in industrial schools and he received his first prison sentence at the age of 15, but as he matured he became more focused. He was regarded as the mastermind behind a £1.7 million heist from a Securicor cash in transit van in Marino Mart in 1987, and later the Brinks

Allied robbery, deemed military in style and netting the gang £3 million, Ireland's biggest robbery at the time.

'Flash' Larry Dunne had earned his nickname. He'd lived it up in a mansion in the hills beyond Dublin City and in chauffeur-driven limos funded by his heroin business. Like the Cahills and the Hutch family, the Dunnes had grown up in abject poverty. Eight brothers were headed up by the eldest, Christy 'Bronco' Dunne, who throughout the 1970s masterminded cash in transit and jewel robberies. Known for violence, the Dunne brothers were entrepreneurial too and in the late 1970s they had taken advantage of a glut of cheap heroin that flooded the drug markets in Europe after the fall of the Shah of Iran. Although most of the family were involved in crime it was Larry who became the most notorious. He was behind the importation of heroin, which was passed on to middlemen before ending up on the streets. Ireland was unprepared for the mass heroin epidemic, and the Gardaí had never before experienced an organised crime gang that ran its drug empire like a business. As a tight-knit family of eight brothers the Dunnes had a blood bond and Bronco once gave an insight into their success. 'With my brothers I felt that if we ever did do anything then it was a closely kept secret between us. We worked together. We could depend on each other with our lives and we knew that whatever we did nobody else would ever know about it.' At one stage Larry is believed to have controlled up to 50 per cent of all heroin trafficking in Ireland and at the height of his notoriety he moved from his small home in Crumlin to a mountainside mansion in Sandyford in south Dublin – a path that was to be followed by many after him. In 1983 he was convicted of possessing and supplying heroin. His first trial ended abruptly with accusations of jury nobbling, but a second jury found him guilty in just 20 minutes after a four-day trial. Dunne wasn't there to hear his fate, though, as he had fled to Spain. He was finally recaptured in 1985 in Portugal and sent back to Ireland to serve his 14-year prison term. As he was led away Larry Dunne famously warned that if anyone thought he was bad, they should see what was coming up behind him. He wasn't wrong.

In the wings, waiting to step into Larry Dunne's shoes, was an ambitious young criminal called Christy Kinahan, an outsider from a middle-class family but with a hunger to learn the workings of gangland. There were others, too – the 'Zombie', the 'Whale' and the 'Colonel' – nicknames as familiar on the streets as they were in the headlines. Their world must have seemed exciting and alluring, their lives dangerous and dramatic as they dodged bullets and faced down the authorities and a State they believed had left them to rot in their own impoverished childhoods. To the young and ambitious they had both wealth and fame; they were the kings of their own fiefdoms. While many of those first-generation armed robbers had diversified into narcotics, for the next to come of age there was only one business in town and that was selling pills and powder, rocks and wraps to a never-ending customer base – a model of growth that seemed to outdo all others.

The big-league criminals whose nicknames graced the front pages of newspapers and who flaunted their enormous wealth seemed to revel in leading the way for the youngsters who brought their product to market. Cannabis was still the most popular drug to buy in the early 1990s, and in Dublin that market had been cornered by the Ballyfermot criminal 'Factory' John Gilligan, who had suppliers in Amsterdam and an army of young teenage dealers to bring his wares to the streets. The eldest of nine children, Gilligan, who hailed from Ballyfermot, had left school at 14 and got a job as a merchant seaman. But he wasn't long for making an honest living and picked up a conviction for larceny a year later. Hijackings and warehouse robberies followed, and his outfit became known as the Factory Gang. He learned about the drug industry in prison, and that was where he met the contacts who helped him source the cannabis resin that would move him up the ladder. The death of The General in 1994 gave him his really big break. Cahill had financed 'Factory' John's first big import but died in a hail of bullets before he could get his cut from the investment, leaving all the profits in Gilligan's hands. As a result of his windfall and his wiped debt he quickly turned that first shipment into a €20 million a year business. His swagger, party-loving lifestyle and brazen spend of that money bought him admiration from the young kids he employed. They included a group of schoolfriends from the Crumlin area of Dublin, who were one of his best sales teams. Crumlin, south of the city, had decent housing stock and lots of settled areas, but pockets of it had been home to some of the most notorious criminals of the previous decades. Among them, Martin 'The Viper' Foley lived on Cashel Avenue, fraudster James 'Jaws' Byrne had moved his family to Raleigh Square, and extortionist James 'The Whale' Gantley resided on Sundrive Road. Gilligan saw that it was the next generation, many of whose parents were part and parcel of criminal networks, who were street smart and tough enough to hold their own while peddling his product. So proud was he of schoolboys Declan Gavin and Brian Rattigan that he took them to the Netherlands to meet his suppliers and promised that they'd become his top lieutenants.

Movement in and out of the country was vital for those who wanted to stay at the top of the ladder. They needed trusted suppliers who could sell them enough bulk through secure routes to enable them to become important wholesalers in the Irish market. It was easy enough to travel to Amsterdam and Málaga, where drug deals were cut with foreign mobs who controlled the entry of Moroccan cannabis, Turkish heroin and a growing supply of Colombian cocaine into Europe. But movement was also risky, and relying on ever more regular business trips became tiresome, so in the 1990s the first of the big-league drug dealers started to find their wings and migrate to Europe in a more permanent way. Forging careers for themselves as wholesalers with the big players from the UK, Russia and South America meant being closer to the action and more bedded down in the cities where business was done. Their presence in the drug centres of Belgium, the Netherlands and on Spain's Costa del Sol meant that there was a guaranteed conveyor belt of guns and drugs for a growing cohort of street gangs further down the ladder.

George 'The Penguin' Mitchell was one of the first to see the need to expand into Europe. In the early 1990s he had been constantly on the move, jetting between Amsterdam, Málaga, Liverpool and Dublin. He needed a base in Europe and in 1994 he moved with his wife, Rebecca Shannon, and a number of their grown-up children to Amsterdam, settling first in the up-market residential street de Watermolen. On 6 June 1996, Tony Gregory named him in the Dáil and described him as a heroin dealer. Under Dáil privilege, Gregory could not be sued for making this claim. But by then he was fully settled in his adopted Dutch city and had set himself up as a legitimate businessman with a number of companies. At that point he was believed to be the kingpin behind an ecstasy-making factory in Dublin, the first of its kind in Ireland, which had been busted before it was about to go into production.

Mitchell, a former truck driver for the Jacobs biscuit company, had come from a modest working-class background, but he was the pioneer of Irish organised crime. Based in Amsterdam but moving around Europe, he'd left strong cell structures behind in Ireland which were to be his bread and butter as he established further markets in the UK and beyond. He had a smooth-running southern branch of his business, nicknamed the Cork Mafia, which had laid claim to the province of Munster; and a strong and loyal business contingent in Dublin led by his brother Paddy and two of his oldest pals, Gerard Hopkins and Stephen Kearney, friends since their early twenties. All looked up to Mitchell and followed his two golden rules of hard work and keeping a modest home. North of the border he had connections with paramilitaries, in particular with the INLA, and he had tight links with Liverpool, a city as important as Amsterdam in the movement of drugs. From his base in Amsterdam he worked on cutting out the middlemen from other mafias and forging his own connections directly with Colombian and Bolivian cartels who could supply him cocaine, a drug he saw as the gold of the future. Mitchell's relocation followed that of his sidekick and long-term business partner Robbie Murphy, who'd moved to Amsterdam around a year earlier and by his senior dealers Thomas 'The Boxer' Mullen, Tommy 'The Zombie' Savage and Derek 'Maradona' Dunne. All had been deemed responsible for the second heroin epidemic and had been the focus of the Concerned Parents group, but their ambition lay way beyond Dublin. Mitchell and Murphy quickly started setting up companies across Europe and investment funds in Denmark, where they felt safe to hold their dirty money. At home, they had buyers desperate for their goods in all corners of the island of Ireland.

The 1990s also saw the rise of Christy 'The Dapper Don' Kinahan Sr, who had firmly set his sights on joining Mitchell as an international player. He partnered up with John 'The Colonel' Cunningham when the pair met behind bars in the late 1980s, when Kinahan was serving his first lengthy sentence for selling heroin. Cunningham was from Ballyfermot and a contemporary of Mitchell. He had a long history in crime, but he'd made a big mistake when he and his brother Michael decided to hop off a wave of IRA kidnappings that had swept Ireland in the 1980s. Looking to make a quick million, the duo had abducted and for eight days held Jennifer Guinness, the wife of the chairman of the Guinness Mahon bank, John Guinness. An all-night siege on upmarket Waterloo Road in Dublin had ended their plan and landed both hefty 17-year terms behind bars. John Cunningham was desperate to make up for his lost years once he got out of prison and Kinahan had a ruthless vision for a place at the very top of global organised crime. On his release in 1991 Kinahan had moved straight into the ecstasy market, buying from Mitchell's network while eyeing up the supply chain from Amsterdam. After another run-in with the law that was set to land him in prison again, he made the jump and moved to the Netherlands and the heart of the action. Cunningham joined him, escaping from Shelton Abbey open prison in 1996 on a day out. They were in prime position in the Netherlands when the biggest player in the cannabis market in Ireland became the victim of his own success.

It was the actions of 'Factory' John Gilligan that really made the 1990s a key decade of change. Police and politicians declared war on Ireland's underworld and dangerous promotion opportunities were opened up for many to move up the gangland ranks before their time and without the wisdom of age. The murder of journalist Veronica Guerin in June 1996 was undoubtedly a seminal moment for the State. She had been working for the *Sunday Independent* and had been writing about John Gilligan and his meteoric rise to riches in a two-year period during which he had flooded the country with cannabis. She had relentlessly pursued Gilligan and in 1995 had been shot in the leg by a masked gunman at the front door of her home. Later that year she had called, alone, to Gilligan's home in the Kildare countryside to confront him, and he had physically attacked her. That incident led to her filing a complaint with the Gardaí and a charge against him was imminent. But on 26 June 1996, as she drove her red Opel Calibra to Dublin from Naas, she was shot six times by two men on a motorbike.

Guerin's murder caused outrage, Taoiseach John Bruton calling it 'an attack on democracy'. The killing instantly turned apathy about the growing threat of organised crime into a tide of hysteria. Police and politicians vowed to wage war on the gangs and for the first time surveillance experts from the Garda's Special Detective Unit were transferred from tracking terrorists to investigating who was who in the criminal underworld. The State reacted quickly. It established the Criminal Assets Bureau (CAB), whose function was to identify assets that had been illegally acquired; and now the burden of proof was on the owner to show they were not the proceeds of crime. The Act establishing CAB was just one of six tough anti-crime bills passed through the Oireachtas in one day. John Bruton, in an address to the Dáil, said that every area of the criminal justice system was being 'modernised with vigour and determination'. He told deputies: 'It is the culmination of the most concentrated month's work on one topic by all arms of government in recent times.' An extra six hundred gardaí would be on the streets, more prison places were to be created, more judges would be appointed, and a referendum would ask people to decide if they wanted to restrict the right to bail. The new Garda Commissioner Pat Byrne suggested locating a Garda liaison officer in Madrid and another in The Hague as part of the battle against the tide of drugs flooding into the country, measures that were approved by Minister for Justice Nora Owen. Extra resources were also poured into the Forensic Science Laboratory to enable it to develop DNA testing and profiling as a huge heave against the Gilligan gang began. It would take years for the effects to be felt, but despite all the changes, the stable door was open and the horse had already bolted. With Mitchell and Kinahan firmly bedded down in the Netherlands and eyeing up bases on the Costa del Sol, a strong Irish-led supply route was by then operating. Stopping the flow of drugs would be like putting a finger in a dam.

While the media and politicians were focused on the new measures being introduced and the fresh commitment to tackle organised crime, none of the headlines or the crackdowns were making much difference to the young and hungry dealers bringing drugs to market. In fact, the only thing that was occupying their minds was the underworld scramble for power that followed the targeting of Gilligan's gang. In the Netherlands Kinahan and Cunningham took the reins while back home in Crumlin, Ballyfermot, Coolock and other parts of the city, newcomers jostled with the old guard for position, seeing the potential to rise from street dealers to wholesalers. While many bigger players swooped in to pick at the bones of Gilligan's cannabis empire, more saw the potential in the phenomenal growth of cocaine use, which had been rising steadily since the beginning of the 1990s in a trajectory that followed the economy.

The murder of Veronica Guerin and the shocking assassination, just months before, of Detective Garda Jerry McCabe were the most high-profile cases being raised in the Dáil, but gun crime among rival gangs had been slowly rising. While the government grappled to restore confidence and catch up on a surge in their activities, gangs had been forming in greater numbers than ever before; and firepower was supplied as easily as the drugs they dealt in. In his report *Homicide in Ireland 1992–1996*, Dr Enda

Dooley, Director of Prison Medical Services of the Department of Justice, Equality and Law Reform, noted that murders with a background of organised crime had replaced those resulting from terrorism. His portion of the study focused on 15 murders described as 'apparently related to disputes concerning control over the supply of illicit drugs and other criminal activity'. Three occurred in 1993, including that of criminal Michael Godfrey; two in 1994, the year Martin 'The General' Cahill was executed; two in 1995; and eight in 1996. Of the cases referenced in the study, 14 incidents had resulted in the death of a single person and one in the death of two individuals. The report focused on what would become an ongoing problem for gardaí investigating a spike in gangland murders to come. According to Dr Dooley's report:

> In all these cases the perpetrator(s) left the scene immediately and made no admission of involvement. This led to an eventual situation where only three of these cases resulted in a conviction (all with murder verdicts). In 7 cases no perpetrator had been detected while in a further 4 cases there was insufficient evidence to charge any suspect. Again . . . this lack of conviction is significantly higher than in the sample as a whole where 118 (57.6%) incidents had resulted in some form of court conviction.

The report continued:

> To a degree the category of 'organised crime related' homicides has replaced those related to terrorist or subversive

motive in this analysis. Both motive types show a number of similarities. The events are usually planned in advance, involve firearms (usually handguns) and are often undertaken with direct and indirect assistance. The suspect is not directly identifiable and usually leaves the scene immediately. Even if a suspect is identified there is no admission of involvement These factors combine to lead to a relatively low conviction rate for these premeditated events.

One criminal, PJ Judge, was a chief suspect in three of the deaths over the study period: Michael Godfrey, who he'd fallen out with; small-time criminal William 'Jock' Corbally, who was understood to have been buried alive; and the killer Michael Brady, who was shot dead in Dublin city centre. While Mitchell and Kinahan were the ambitious and ruthless businessmen at the top of the tree, the likes of Judge was exactly the type of psychopath drawn to the world of wealth and power that they facilitated. Before the end of the report period, and months after the killing of Guerin, Judge himself became a murder statistic. Nicknamed 'Psycho', Judge operated in north Dublin, where he controlled a vast chunk of the drug trade. He'd been violent since he was a child and as a teenager had shot up a rival's home after stealing a gun. During an armed robbery he shot a postmaster and tried to kill an unarmed garda. Judge terrorised everyone who came into his sphere and was capable of killing anyone for any slight, such was his paranoia. He executed Godfrey because of a drug deal that had gone wrong. In 1996 he kidnapped and executed Corbally for no better reason than envy of his good looks and popularity. Brady, who'd brutally killed his own wife, had been shot dead on behalf of Judge's underling Martin 'Marlo' Hyland, whose sister was Brady's wife. Hyland should have been grateful, but he was more ambitious than Judge could ever have guessed, and he was braver too. On 7 December 1996 Judge was shot dead at point-blank range as he got into his car outside the Royal Oak pub in Finglas. The execution benefited many, but in particular Hyland, who immediately moved in to take over his boss's old turf and who would go on to become even more notorious.

Months after the murder of Guerin, John Gilligan was picked up at Heathrow Airport and found to be carrying a suitcase of cash. He was placed in custody while the probe into his involvement in the journalist's death continued. His lieutenant Paul Ward was already behind bars and facing a murder charge but was defiant in the face of the State's new get-tough attitude. He was adamant he would beat the rap and make as much noise about his innocence as he could. Ward took little time in befriending one of the country's most volatile criminals and together they hatched a plan. Warren Dumbrell was just 22 years old but was already notorious when he was jailed for robbing a corner shop, and he palled up with Ward behind bars. Dumbrell was the first son of Colin and Margaret Dumbrell, a union that had resulted in a brood of bloodthirsty brothers whose violent impulses had resulted in them becoming some of the most feared criminals both inside and outside the prison system. Colin had already built up an impressive criminal record by the time his first, and most infamous, son Warren was born on 23 April 1974 at St James's Hospital in Dublin. Unlike many residents of the drug-ridden

O'Devaney Gardens flat complex where he then lived, Colin had not grown up in the tenements but had come from a relatively affluent family; his father William was a salesman and his mother Evelyn a housewife. He had completed his schooling, unlike so many who entered crime at that time, and was proud to tell anyone who would listen that he chose a life of crime and was not born into it. He was just 24 when Margaret brought baby Warren home to Flat 283 and was already known to the Garda Síochána as a violent bully who would turn his hand to anything to make a quick buck. The couple had six more children and moved to Inchicore where, as a young teenager, Warren suffered a terrible accident that would leave him disfigured for life. One day after school he and a group of pals were playing a game of 'skutting' – hitching a ride on the back of one of the Guinness stout lorries that passed along the busy streets. But when it came to Warren's turn he lost his footing and fell. As his friends looked on in horror, Warren was hit by a truck and fell under the wheel, which rolled over his head, smashing his skull. In 1989, aged just 15 and still recovering, Warren went on his first crime spree, racking up ten convictions for burglary, road traffic offences and stealing. By 16 he managed to clock up another six convictions, the most serious of which was for possession of a firearm. Constantly in and out of prison, he continued his life of crime, becoming more and more violent, even to the most frail and innocent members of society.

Just how deeply Warren had grown to hate authority became frighteningly apparent in the New Year of 1997. In custody in Mountjoy Prison and partnered up with Paul Ward, he planned and carried out what was known as the Siege of Mountjoy.

Tensions in what was then Ireland's largest prison were high; it was also totally overcrowded, with up to three prisoners in a cell sharing a bucket as a toilet and having to slop out in the mornings. Warren was particularly furious about the way he was being treated and his anger was shared by Ward, who was raging that he was facing a murder rap when the rest of the Gilligan gang had gone on the run. Together they decided that they would teach the warders and Governor John Lonergan a lesson. Over a number of days they gathered supporters and decided to hold a rooftop protest which, they wagered, would be watched by the nation and would embarrass the prison staff, the Gardaí and the Department of Justice. Shortly before 5.50pm on 4 January 1997, Warren, Ward and their gang were moved to the separation unit of the prison for their evening's recreation. This was where the prison authorities placed the most volatile of inmates and those who had repeatedly caused trouble or arguments with fellow prisoners. It was an ordinary Saturday, or so the officers thought. Hidden under his clothing Dumbrell had a stainless steel knife. He had syringes too, and one of his gang had a razor blade – weapons of terror they had squirreled away in the run-up to their attack. But the plan would fall at the first hurdle. One of the team had managed to break through a ceiling but they couldn't get any higher because of the prison's concrete roof. Instead they took four prison officers hostage and then a fifth who came to investigate what was going on. Together they held syringes filled with hepatitis-infected blood to the necks of their captives and told them, 'I'll make you drink my blood.' (Hepatitis and AIDS were huge problems in the system at the time, and many prisoners were infected. The mere threat was enough to strike fear into the prison officers.) They forced the prison officers to kneel on the ground as though they were about to be executed. As he taunted them, Dumbrell squirted blood from his syringe. Ward threatened to hang them with a rope made from duvet covers, making them stand on tables, which he threatened to kick out from under them. Over and over again they held the syringes to the officer's necks, telling them they would infect them. The siege continued for 53 hours as the pair acted out their own real-life horror movie. Eventually the Department of Justice agreed to investigate the complaints in an attempt to defuse the worst hostage crisis in the history of the prison service. One by one the terrorised officers were released and brought straight to hospital to be examined for injuries and to be treated for trauma. In ordered society the scenes were abhorrent; in the lawless underworld Dumbrell and Ward were heroes.

In the meantime Gilligan gang member Brian Meehan was lifted in Amsterdam as moves began to extradite him, while gardaí managed to turn two others, Charlie Bowden and Russell Warren, into supergrass witnesses for the upcoming trials. In January 1998 the trial of Paul Ward opened at the Special Criminal Court, while extradition proceedings against Meehan and Gilligan continued. In November Ward was convicted of Veronica Guerin's murder. Prosecutors admitted that he was not the triggerman but argued that he should be held equally liable for the reporter's murder as he had disposed of the handgun and motorcycle that were used in the hit. Critical to Ward's conviction was the evidence of his former associate Bowden, the first time in the legal history of the Irish Republic that the court would accept uncorroborated testimony as the basis for a conviction. Seven months later Ward was sentenced to 12 years for his part in the Siege of Mountjoy.

While the Ward murder conviction would be overturned, the trial in the Special Criminal Court revealed another weapon in the State's new armoury against organised crime. The court had been established in the 1970s, just after the Troubles in Northern Ireland began, to try Provisional IRA volunteers before three judges, with no jury; this was to negate the risk of light sentences and to prevent jury-tampering. But the Guerin murder case led to its remit being extended to drug gangs and criminals. In June 1999 Brian Meehan went on trial denying murder and 16 other drug- and weapons-related charges. He would become the only man convicted of her murder.

In Belmarsh Prison, three years into his fight against his extradition, John Gilligan was knee-deep in law books in his cell writing a writ of habeas corpus to the Divisional Court in London in an eleventh-hour bid to stop authorities sending him back to Ireland. The legal argument was that since no three-judge court existed in the UK with the same powers as Dublin's Special Criminal Court, he couldn't be extradited to Ireland to face such a court. But his appeal fell on deaf ears and in February 2000 he appeared in the Dublin courts on Green Street charged with Guerin's murder after being flown in by an Air Corps CASA jet from RAF Northolt in England. The High Court in London had dismissed his appeal against extradition.

One month later the effects of his undoing, and that of his associates, the publicity around his downfall and the example made of him by the State made zero difference to his former employees. In March of that year the rise and ambition of his former schoolboy protégés was laid bare when gardaí raided a room of the Holiday Inn on Pearse Street in Dublin and discovered 18-year-old Graham Whelan and 20-year-old Philip Griffiths cutting cocaine valued at €750,000 and €500,000 worth of ecstasy. It was business as usual. While the pair were caught red-handed with the drugs, their boss, Declan Gavin, was asleep in another room and was not charged. Gavin and Brian Rattigan had had an uneasy relationship for a long time, but the paranoia around Gavin's stroke of good fortune in the Holiday Inn would set Gilligan's former gang members on a murderous feud for the next ten years. Around the same time a decision in the UK by the Home Office considering the release of a violent inmate, Wayne Dundon, would create a parallel feud in Limerick where warring gangs were also oblivious to the Garda's crackdown on crime. Despite the politicians' and Garda's fighting talk, the new millennium would create a growing need for enforcers and for killers as the violent old guard made way for a new and more ruthless one.

As the population of gangland burgeoned amidst a perfect storm of financial growth, marginalisation and ambition, job opportunities in organised crime opened up for greater numbers than ever before. Cold and emotionless business brains sat in Europe at the very top of the tree dealing with heroin, cannabis and cocaine suppliers. Wearing suits and posing as legitimate business people, they organised shipments and worked out innovative ways to launder dirty money. Below them were the layers of wholesalers, logistics experts and financiers who helped move the product and money across the continent and into Ireland. In towns and cities across the country various gangs and criminal cell structures waited to bring the goods to a dog-eat-dog marketplace where control and fear were the most important ingredients for success. While many of the groupings of young men were fluid, sometimes only coming together for robberies or armed heists, the underworld became much more structured than before. With the existence of CAB and its deeper reach into the pockets of criminals, money launderers and those with ideas on how to hide cash found themselves enjoying elevated importance in the minds of mob bosses anxious to keep the State's hands off their dirty cash. Those with a mind for business and a natural ability to understand profits and losses were also in demand, from street level to higher positions as senior lieutenants. Logistics experts were vital cogs, too, as they arranged the movement of drugs and cash. But while the white-collar accountants of the underworld counted the money and moved the funds, the real boom was in the harder side of criminality, which needed enforcers and debt collectors. And it was in those vast housing estates constructed at pace to alleviate tenement squalor, built around courtyards, towering 15 storeys high, lined around large green fields and divided with laneways, cul-de-sacs and rat runs, where children were schooled in the business of death.

CHAPTER TWO

A Killing Boom

By the turn of the new millennium two major feuds which would together claim more than 35 lives were under way in Limerick and Dublin. Both were dubbed "cocaine wars", but the reality was that the gangs of Limerick and Dublin were also at war in a battle for supremacy in a world dominated by alpha males intent on winning their turf. Both feuds played out in small geographical areas where opportunities were rarely overlooked and a 'fight to the death' mentality provided a decade of work for hitmen paid handsomely for their services.

Like Dublin, Limerick had its share of social problems and the Dooley report had, designated it, along with the capital, a murder blackspot. Similar to the housing problems in Dublin, Limerick had concentrated large populations of uneducated and unemployed people in its city estates, resulting in high incidences of crime, addiction and disadvantage. Of the almost 20,000 houses in the city area, more than 8,000 were built by the council. First came St Mary's Park, known as the Island Field, built in 1934 to house those who'd been living in city slums. Throughout the 1970s and 1980s, in response to population growth, areas like Moyross and Southhill sprang up and became home to those who, even as the jobs came, were five times more likely to be unemployed than the national average. It was in an even more marginalised sector of society within that social exclusion, the Travelling community, that a marriage would create a band of brothers whose mark will remain on the city of Limerick long after they are gone.

Storm clouds surely gathered when Limerick couple Kenneth Dundon and Anne McCarthy wed in a ceremony in Hackney in London in 1982, an alliance which would spawn a murderous family unrivalled anywhere in Irish criminal history. The couple had met while still in school but married in the UK after fleeing Limerick, where Kenneth had survived a shooting incident. Both came from families hardened by drink and violence and each already had a long history of trouble with the law before their romance began. Kenneth, in particular, had a reputation for extreme and uncontrolled aggression; his first conviction for assault, in Limerick, dated back to 1974. Theirs was a stormy and violent relationship fuelled by severe alcohol dependency. After the marriage five sons had followed in quick succession; first came Wayne in 1978, then Dessie in 1981 followed by John, Gerard, Kenny Jr and finally Annabel, the youngest and the only girl in the male-dominated family. There is little doubt but the Dundons were hardened from the crib and left to fend for themselves, and the only way they appeared to gain approval from their father was through violence. There were no boundaries when it came to giving a rival, or an innocent civilian, a severe beating. Wayne, Dessie, John and Gerard were in trouble with the law from a very early age and the family were the scourge of the local police in London who, when they were not prising Kenneth and Anne apart during their vicious arguments, were chasing after the boys for house burglary or violent assaults.

The eldest son, Wayne, decided that he would set the bar for the rest to follow. He never smoked, drank or took drugs – his true addiction was inflicting pain. At one point as a young teenager he gave his own mother such a severe beating she had to be hospitalised for weeks. Those who came into contact with him over the years describe a menace that radiates from him and cold blue eyes that are said to be completely vacant and show absolutely no emotion. His white, almost translucent, skin only colours with rage and when angry he regularly froths at the mouth. A top bare-knuckle street fighter, he was gifted with a punch of both speed and strength and from the outset he was unquestionably the head of his family. At 18 years of age Wayne was jailed for four years for a series of robberies from elderly people. During one he savagely beat a wheelchair-bound pensioner and in another he robbed and terrorised a 90-year-old woman. His choice of vulnerable victims who were unable to fight back meant that when he was due for release from prison, the UK's Home Office, the government department responsible for passports, crime, counter-terrorism and immigration, considered him so dangerous that it took the extraordinary step of deporting him back to Ireland.

In the years that followed, the entire Dundon clan followed him back to their native Limerick and to the city centre social housing estate of Ballinacurra Weston where brothers Wayne, Dessie and John managed to get neighbouring houses on the main Hyde Road. In Limerick their cousins in the McCarthy mob were already a recognised crime family who had gone to war with brothers Kieran and Christy Keane and their gang who, along with members of the Collopy grouping, controlled most of the lucrative drug supply into Limerick. Cousins Anthony 'Noddy' McCarthy, Larry McCarthy Jr and James McCarthy had already begun to get a small foothold in the drugs trade and were prepared to do anything to catch up with the Keane–Collopy outfit and snatch their business. The Dundons' arrival gave the McCarthys the backup they needed to really show their rivals what they were made of and as tensions grew a deep-seated mentality of clan warfare set in. Familial groupings with blood ties, which had long been the backbone of some of the most notorious of the earliest Irish mobs, were all too evident in Limerick and this was something that would challenge police into the new era of an ever more violent gangland.

The concept of blood loyalty that Bronco Dunne had described years before was familiar throughout the world: the Genna crime family, the Sicilian mafia of Chicago, was headed up by six brothers; in New York the Gambinos and Genoveses were made up of siblings and cousins drawn together; in the UK the Adams Family, or the A team, led by brothers Terry, Sean and Patrick terrorised Islington through drug trafficking and extortion and racking up more than twenty murders. Not long after the arrival of the Dundon brothers from England an incident within the Keane mob would light a spark of the violence to come when Eddie Ryan, the one-time enforcer for the Keane–Collopy mob, was gunned down at the city's Moose Bar. He'd once worked for the gang but had become unhappy with his minor role. He'd tried to kill Christy Keane, but the gun jammed and his own death warrant was signed. After his death the younger generations took on the fight and tensions between the sons of Eddie Ryan and the second-generation Keanes bubbled over. Unknown to them, the Dundons were watching the developments with interest and identifying a complex way to use Ryan's grieving sons to stamp out their opposition.

Wayne Dundon meant business from the moment he returned to Limerick. In 2001 he sanctioned a hit on his own cousin John Creamer when there was a row over the proceeds of a jewel shop robbery, proving that he could turn on anyone who crossed him. Creamer was shot 15 times by an assassin but survived. Throughout that year there were dozens of shooting incidents linked to Dundon, but no fatalities. Wayne and his brothers ran roughshod over the neighbourhood of Ballinacurra Weston, where they took total control. They'd pull young men from their beds and set them to work for them in whatever way they needed; they used their powerful fists to pulverise anyone who refused their bidding; and they created a fortified compound between their three houses, running neighbours from their homes and using the vacant buildings as stash houses for their drugs or lookouts for gardaí. In 2002 the murder of innocent bouncer Brian Fitzgerald terrified the city of Limerick and showed police what the Dundons were capable of. The killing was ordered because Fitzgerald had stood up to Wayne Dundon and refused to allow the family's drugs to be sold in the popular nightclub Docs, where he was head of security.

As the months wore on the Dundons strengthened their ties with their cousins, the McCarthys, and eyed up an opportunity to take a big scalp from the Keane–Collopy grouping. In January 2003 Kieran Ryan and Eddie Ryan Jr, sons of the murdered enforcer Eddie Ryan Sr, were reported to have been abducted from a street in Limerick and bundled into a car. With tensions between the Ryan and Keane outfits at fever pitch the Gardaí feared a double fatality, and the army was immediately drafted in on suspicion that the brothers were going to be tortured and killed. Despite the speed of the Gardaí's reaction and the resources pumped into the situation, hopes that the brothers would ever be found alive were beginning to fade. Then events took a sensational twist when Kieran Keane and his nephew Owen Treacy went missing too. Then the Ryan brothers showed up, unharmed, after being released by their captors and were photographed celebrating with family and friends. Soon after, the body of Keane and the seriously injured Treacy were discovered at Drombanna, a few miles outside Limerick. In a spectacular double-cross, the Dundons had orchestrated the entire event. It emerged that Keane and Treacy had agreed to attend a pre-arranged meeting at which they thought they'd be liaising with those who'd taken the volatile Ryans. (Despite the Dundons' efforts, brothers Kieran and Philip Collopy hadn't taken the bait.) When Keane and Treacy arrived at the isolated roadside they were jumped on by Dessie

Dundon, James and Anthony McCarthy and two others. Keane was tortured, then shot in the head. Treacy was stabbed 17 times and left for dead on the roadside. Miraculously, he survived to give evidence against the five-man team who had plotted the narco-style attack. John Dundon was already behind bars for threatening to kill Treacy when Dessie got a life sentence for murder, along with his four co-accused. At the same time Gerard 'Ger' Dundon got a sentence for breaching bail and later for violent disorder and threatening a witness. A year later Wayne joined his brothers when he got a ten-year sentence for threatening to kill a barman. The Dundons' sister Annabel had been just 14 years old when she was refused entrance to Brannigan's pub by barman Ryan Lee. Infuriated, Wayne had cocked his fingers in the shape of a gun, pushed them against Lee's face and warned him: 'Fuck you, you're dead.' Nineteen-year-old Lee was shot just half an hour after the incident at the pub. The owner of the bar, Roy Collins, would later be gunned down in retaliation for the same incident.

The years that followed would shine a light on the level of violence the Dundons were capable of inflicting, but they also give an insight into the types of hitmen they unearthed in the city and beyond. Like other high-profile gang bosses, Wayne and John Dundon found themselves so heavily surveilled that, even though they were capable of murder, they had to hire freelances to carry out their bidding to keep themselves at arm's length from the crime. Limerick, like Dublin, had a history steeped in IRA activity but was also the southern headquarters of the dissident grouping Continuity IRA. It had been established in 1986 after a split in the Provisional IRA but had been very active since

1994 when it began a campaign in Northern Ireland against the British Army and the PSNI. The links between Limerick and the North provided a supply route for guns and easy access to firearms training for those interested in the art of killing.

Gary Campion first came to public attention in 2006 when he was charged, along with a number of other men, with the 2002 murder of Brian Fitzgerald, the 34-year-old father of two who had refused to let the McCarthy–Dundon gang sell drugs in the nightclub where he worked as head of security. He would likely have got away with it were it not for English contract killer James Cahill, who confessed to the murder. Before he was jailed for life Cahill implicated Campion and John Dundon in the killing. He gave evidence in court outlining how Campion drove him to and from the murder scene on a motorbike, a job for which he was paid €10,000. Cahill was an unusual character. He hailed from Birmingham but had been brought up in County Clare, where he came into contact with associates of the Dundon mob. He was just 30 when he was hired by the Dundon gang and had already had previous convictions for firearms offences. He'd gone to Fitzgerald's house at Brookhaven Walk in Corbally in the early hours one morning and, along with Campion, lay in wait for him in the bushes, pouncing when Fitzgerald returned home from work. Fitzgerald fought with the pair, then a number of shots were fired and he fell to the ground, injured, and tried to crawl away. Cahill pursued him and shot him in the back of the head. In prison Cahill had had a road to Damascus moment, sparked by fear that he was going to be killed, and from his cell in Portlaoise had asked to speak to gardaí, telling them: 'They are going to kill me.' He made a request to be transferred to a more secure location before he confessed to the murder and named Campion and others involved. He told gardaí: 'I shot him and no one else. I want to get this out of my system, I want to get this out in the open.' Despite Cahill's desire for his co-conspirators to pay the price for the murder of Fitzgerald, John Dundon was acquitted of the crime.

Campion, however, was convicted and jailed for life in 2007. In the periods of freedom he'd enjoyed before going to prison, he'd been kept busy. Just four weeks after the killing of Fitzgerald, he'd played a role in the McCarthy–Dundons' murder of car dealer Seán Poland during a botched robbery at his home in County Clare on New Year's Eve. Campion, who was only 19 at the time, and another man had soon emerged as chief suspects. Less than five months later, Campion was implicated in the murder of Robert Fitzgerald, a 23-year-old who was shot in the head because he'd associated with people in the Keane–Collopy gang. In 2006 Campion shot 'Fat' Frankie Ryan, a member of the McCarthy–Dundon gang, in a personal dispute, which angered his paymasters. A judge struck out that high-profile murder case a year later, but Campion's brother Noel was shot dead by the Dundons in revenge, and he was soon in the dock on the Fitzgerald murder.

While remorseful killers like Cahill, plagued by voices in their head and a terrible desire to confess, are rare, gunmen like Campion are far more typical of the type of hitman that gangs can find in the impoverished communities where they operate. Like Campion, many are both organised and disorganised criminals, often capable of killing either to order or on a whim. Their backgrounds are often steeped in violence and in most cases they have come from troubled homes. Campion came from a family entrenched in violence. His brother William Jr was sentenced to life in prison for the murder of Patrick Skehan, a 68-year-old bachelor farmer from County Clare who was found beaten and unconscious in his home, his hands and legs bound with cable wire, hanging upside down from the bannisters. Another brother, Noel, was a convicted armed robber. Gary started out robbing cars and selling drugs but soon got weapons training and found he was handy with a gun. He was only 19 when he became the chief suspect in the Poland killing. Campion enjoyed the kill and in 2000 he abducted two Limerick brothers, stripped them and was about to shoot them when gardaí arrived. In another case he made so many attempts to kill a young man that the target was so terrified that he took his own life.

Many killers, like Campion, travel to Eastern Europe to learn how to use a gun; others are trained by the IRA terrorists who have gone before them. Ireland is steeped in expertise when it comes to sourcing weapons and using them, thanks to the Troubles in the North and the twisted job opportunities it brought. And while the Provisional IRA would never admit to training killers for anything other than the cause, or having anything to do with the world of drug dealing, many of its members found a good source of income by passing on their skills in bomb-making, gun handling and crime scene destruction methods. One criminal godfather made a career as a murder coach teaching his young protégés everything he knew, from destroying evidence to dismembering and burying bodies. Sean Hunt, nicknamed 'The

Smuggler', was an IRA boss who moonlighted as a pigeon fancier and pet store owner. He first took Eric 'Lucky' Wilson under his wing when he met the psychopathic killer in his native Ballyfermot. He acted as an agent for him and trained his older brother John and his younger brother Keith, along with their cousin Alan and, later, a nephew, Luke. The story of the Wilson clan and their incredible family business would send chills down the spine of the most hardened investigator. Reared in Ballyfermot, where the likes of 'Factory' John GIlligan, John 'The Colonel' Cunningham and George 'The Penguin' Mitchell had started their empires, the boys were brought up by their mother and were long rumoured to have been fathered by Martin 'The General' Cahill, a notorious womaniser who romanced three sisters and had children with all three.

Hunt had an eye for a natural born killer and he took the fatherless Eric under his wing, teaching him the mechanisms of a gun, how to shoot a moving target and how to flee the scene of a kill. Eric had a reputation as being cold-blooded and by the time he walked into the home of his one-time best friend and shot him dead beside his girlfriend, he was fully skilled in the craft of murder. Eric was only 21 when he fell out with his childhood pal Martin Kenny and he was out to settle a score when he broke into Kenny's girlfriend's family home and appeared at the end of their bed at 5am. The killing put Eric firmly in the sights of a notorious criminal sadist known as Mark 'The Guinea Pig' Desmond, a cousin of Kenny, who vowed to take revenge on his killer. Desmond was one of the most feared figures in the Ballyfermot area where he lived and ruled. He was behind a string of murders, including the double assassination of 19-year-old Patrick Murray and 20-year-old Darren Carey, whose bodies were discovered in January 2000 in the Grand Canal in Kildare – killings that would serve as a macabre message of what was to lie ahead in the new millennium. Desmond, then 24, had carried out the killing himself. He was known as a dealer and an enforcer who raped teenage boys as a way of controlling them and terrifying them into collecting his debts and dealing his drugs. He was notorious in his community, as had been his father before him – he was known as a violent bully and a close associate of 'The General'. Eric Wilson was wary rather than afraid when Desmond let it be known that he was going to avenge his cousin's death. Wilson moved away for a cooling-off period, on the advice of his mentor, 'The Smuggler' Hunt, and lay low until the dust settled.

A year after killing his best pal, Eric had picked up work from Finglas drug trafficker Martin 'Marlo' Hyland. A decade after his former boss PJ 'Psycho' Judge was taken out, Hyland had built an even bigger empire for himself in Finglas, a suburb of north Dublin. Hyland had specialised in armed robberies using a network of young criminals known as the 'Filthy Fifty' who he'd hire for jobs and pay them according to the profits made or the success of the robberies. He'd used the money to purchase large amounts of drugs, including cocaine and heroin, and in the ten years since the murder of Judge in 1996, he'd become so powerful and rich that gardaí had set up a special task force to target him. Called Operation Oak, the multi-pronged move against Marlo Hyland had sprung out of a wider Garda initiative called Operation Anvil, established in 2005 to tackle Dublin's gun crime, which had identified just how massive Hyland's operation had become. Throughout 2006 the Hyland network was torn apart by countless arrests and charges brought against 20 members of his inner circle. More than €20 million worth of drugs had been seized, along with guns. As his paranoia grew, Hyland's ferocious temper turned on his own. In 2006 he hired Eric 'Lucky' Wilson to carry out the murder of a County Louth drug dealer, Paul Reay, who he suspected of being a Garda informer and therefore part of his ongoing problems. Despite being mentored by Hunt, who was notoriously clever with money, 'Lucky' Wilson accepted a kilo of cocaine as payment for the cold-blooded killing. As Hyland's gang continued to crumble he desperately clung onto his power, networking with the McCarthy–Dundon gang in Limerick and arranging the shocking murder of mother of two Baiba Saulite, for a man who wanted her dead. Hyland himself would end the year dead in a bed in Scribblestown Park in Finglas, where he was shot as he slept. That attack also claimed the life of an innocent young plumber, Anthony Campbell, aged 20, who was working in the house when the killers came for Hyland. Ironically, Hyland's bloody demise came in exactly the same way as his rise had – through the ambition of an underling. A decade after Hyland had taken over his murdered boss Judge's turf, Eamon 'The Don' Dunne had moved in to get rid of the old guard and take his throne.

Eric 'Lucky' Wilson was an odd, lonely character who was a prolific user of cocaine, which marred his judgement when it came to his work. In 2007 he shot the criminal Roy Coddington, who was under threat of arrest, because he feared he would reveal his involvement in the Reay killing. In confirmation that the carefully balanced underworld operates just like a game of chess and that every move means a shift in position for others, the murder of Coddington would spark significant power changes in the drugs landscape that would have far-reaching effects into the future. Coddington was, along with Reay, the other big supplier in Meath and as a direct result of the two murders a merger of two groups would fill the power vacuum.

Traveller brothers Owen and Brendan Maguire had ruled a patch in the Drogheda area of Louth and had long-standing links with Cornelius Price, who lived in a compound in Gormanston in County Meath. With Coddington out of the way the two groupings, who had similar backgrounds, saw an opportunity to up their supply chain and increase their importance by working together. They quickly moved in to mop up the spoils, forming an alliance that would be marked out in blood.

After the Meath murders of Coddington and Reay, 'Lucky' Wilson moved to Spain, where 'The Smuggler' Hunt helped him find an isolated farmhouse in Coín, where he based himself while offering up his services as a killer. Hunt let the mobs know that 'Lucky' was available for business in Ireland or Spain. The Kinahan organised crime group (OCG), based in nearby Puerto Banús, always needed a skilled killer and he soon picked up a number of jobs for them, including a trusted role in a hit on career criminal Paddy Doyle in 2008. Doyle was himself on the lam in Spain, where he'd been living for three years. A notorious figure in the Irish criminal underworld, he had been the personal hitman and enforcer-in-chief for 'Fat' Freddie Thompson throughout his murderous feud with rival Brian Rattigan in the Crumlin and Drimnagh areas of south-west Dublin. Rattigan and Thompson had once been friends, but they had gone to war after their gang split and both took leadership roles in what was Ireland's first real cocaine war. Doyle fled Ireland in November 2005 after carrying out the murders of Noel Roche, Darren Geoghegan and Gavin Byrne in just two days. While Roche was a rival of Thompson, Geoghegan and Byrne were not – they believed they were meeting Doyle to discuss a drugs delivery. Instead, the cool, calculated killer had got into the back seat of their car and shot both in the back of the head at point-blank range with a 9mm pistol. Doyle had already proved himself a willing assassin when in 2002 he'd murdered 18-year-old Timothy Rattigan outside his home. He had also shot Brian Rattigan that same year in his bed, leaving him injured and having to wear a colostomy bag. Months later Rattigan's beloved younger brother Joey was shot dead after celebrating his 18th birthday.

Doyle had the typical personality of a hitman: he was a wild card and feared nobody. He was unpredictable and impulsive, which, for many, made time spent in his company fun. In Spain, his disrespectful attitude angered mob boss Daniel Kinahan, the heir to the throne Christy Kinahan Sr had built following his ambitious rise from gangland nobody to mafia-style boss. When Doyle was accused of both owing money and being a liability, his fate was sealed. On the day of his murder he was double-crossed by his two best friends, friends he believed he could trust with his life, Freddie Thompson and his childhood pal Gary Hutch. Hutch, a nephew of the legendary criminal Gerry 'The Monk'

Hutch, was living his best life on the Costa after merging with the Kinahan grouping and forging a close friendship with Daniel Kinahan, which had seen him elevated to senior lieutenant in the mob. Although he had known Doyle since they were schoolboys and knew his parents, Gary Hutch was prepared to personally oversee the murder as a measure of his loyalty to Kinahan.

Daniel Kinahan sat down with Thompson and Hutch to plan the end of Doyle so they could make it look like another mob had carried it out. Thompson and Hutch needed to be with Doyle when he came under fire, Kinahan suggested, so there could be no rumours that it had been an in-house job. After making an agreement with 'Lucky' Wilson to pull the trigger, the intricate conspiracy was put together and it was planned to lure Doyle out so that 'Lucky' could strike. Hutch and Thompson knew Doyle well and when they arranged for the electricity to be turned off at his Spanish home they were confident that he would quickly get bored and phone them to arrange a rendezvous. Sure enough, within minutes of the power cut, Doyle called the pair and asked them to collect him so they could go to the gym until his power was back. Hutch drove the car while Thompson chatted to Doyle. Then they stopped at a pre-arranged place and 'Lucky' appeared on the pavement outside the bar and started to shoot into the 4x4. As the bullets flew, Hutch and Thompson abandoned the vehicle and Doyle died in a hail of gunfire. Within hours of his death the Kinahans filtered out word that Doyle had been killed by a Turkish gang angered that he owed them money. To confirm the story they even sent Gary Hutch home with money to pay for his funeral and carry his coffin. In Spain, 'Lucky' Wilson returned to

Coín, where he bedded down in his lonely farmhouse and waited for his next payday.

Months later Doyle's younger brother Barry, raw with grief and terrified that he'd be targeted too, took solace in the arms of the McCarthy–Dundon mob in Limerick. He knew Ger Dundon, the youngest of the brothers, and gambled that he'd be safe under their protection. But it wasn't long before they turned him into a killer too. Years into their murderous feud with the rival Keane–Collopy gang, the older Dundon brothers, Wayne and John, had not satisfied their blood lust, and they ordered the murder of John 'Pitchfork' McNamara. Doyle had enjoyed their protection, used their drugs and stayed at their homes but in the Dundons' world nothing in life comes free and this was time for him to pay back his debt. Fuelled by a cocktail of drugs, Doyle was no skilled marksman and when he was delivered to the neighbourhood where McNamara lived he panicked and shot the wrong man. Instead of the intended target, he killed the innocent rugby player Shane Geoghegan, a murder that would shock the country and result in a renewed crackdown on the mobs of Limerick. In custody, he admitted to the murder during his 15th interview and as he did, he took a pair of rosary beads from his neck, a memento of his dead brother, and asked gardaí to give them to the grieving Geoghegan family as a mark of his remorse. He was 26 years old when he was handed down a life sentence.

Back home another Wilson was appearing on the Garda radar. 'Lucky's' cousin Alan was about to prove that bad blood ran through his veins too. In 2008 a teenage beggar girl was lured into a car on the promise of a McDonald's meal. She disappeared after making a panicked call to her family back in Romania. Marioara Rostas had just arrived in Dublin and she had little English and no way of knowing where she was when she told a relative she'd been kidnapped and was being held in a house. Alan Wilson's best pal Fergus O'Hanlon would later lead officers to a house in the south inner city and then to Mariorora's body buried deep in the Dublin mountains, wrapped tightly in plastic and bound with duct tape. Wilson would be tried but acquitted of the crime, whispering 'thank you' to the jury who found him not guilty. Within months he'd have murder on his mind again.

In Spain 'Lucky' Wilson wasn't out of work for too long. Drug dealer Micka 'The Panda' Kelly, one of the most prominent bosses of the underworld, knew he needed a reliable and violent assassin when he cooked up a plan to kill a drug debt as well as two prolific dealers who had been demanding payment from him. Kelly, who had a big drug operation in Coolock, had been feuding with Belfast drug traffickers David 'Babyface' Lindsay and his associate Alan Napper for months. They were insistent that he pay them up to a million quid for a drug shipment that had gone awry. Kelly decided to call their bluff and made arrangements to meet the pair in a house in rural County Down where he said he would bring the cash. Making his way north from Dublin, Wilson flew to Belfast on a false passport and followed directions to the house, where he bedded down and lay in wait. When the two arrived at the pre-arranged location, Wilson shot them both. Later, he and Kelly cut up their bodies with a chainsaw and buried them. They have never been found.

'Lucky' made his way back to Spain again while 'The Smuggler' Hunt negotiated his next job. Hunt had never seen so much business from a single family. He guided all the Wilson boys, regularly finding jobs for them through a network of connections that spanned the Republic and Northern Ireland. As part of his 'agent' role he allowed them to use his luxury villa in Spain as a place to lie low after hits — and the holiday became part of their pay. Eldest brother John was just 24 when he worked as a getaway driver in the murder of Simon Doyle in West Dublin, a role brokered by Hunt. The third brother, Keith, was contracted to murder Daniel Gaynor, himself a hot-tempered hitman who'd been responsible for at least four murders. Gaynor had lived and died by the gun but had fallen foul of Eamon 'The Don' Dunne, who was fast becoming the biggest employer of killers in town.

Not only had Dunne's takeover of his former boss Hyland's business been ruthless, but he had brought to it an even more paranoid and dangerous attitude than before. Dunne was an associate of Hunt and trusted him to provide him with proficient guns for hire over a murderous four-year reign as the northside's most feared gang boss. In 2009 he employed 'Lucky' Wilson to help him solve a problem in Spain. Christy Gilroy had worked as a hitman for Dunne in the ruthless double murders of Michael 'Roly' Cronin and James Maloney at Summerhill in Dublin. Cronin was a heroin dealer accused of being one of George 'The Penguin' Mitchell's biggest wholesalers in the north inner city. Dunne was no community activist and didn't care about the damage that was being done by heroin, but he wanted the dealers out of the way in revenge for perceived slights to him. Gilroy was himself hooked on heroin and made mistakes during the kill. He'd arranged to meet Cronin and Maloney under the pretence of doing a drug deal and had got into the back of their car to shoot them both, but in the panic of the getaway he'd thrown the murder weapon and his clothing under a car close to the crime scene. They'd been found by gardaí and held as forensic evidence that could link Gilroy to the double murder, which would in turn jeopardise Dunne as his employer.

After the murders Gilroy had been flown out to Spain to get specialist treatment for his addiction, but Dunne had instead got 'Lucky' Wilson to collect him, kill him and disappear his body. What happened next would prove how 'Lucky's' lonely and sinister existence in the farmhouse at Coín had turned him into a monster in every sense of the word. Aged just 26, Wilson was on a night out in the Lounge Bar in Riviera del Sol, near Mijas, in 2010 when he groped a young girl. British tourist Dan Smith, who was 24, told Wilson to stop and the pair pushed and shoved one another around the bar before 'Lucky' fled on a motorbike, vowing to return to finish the fight. The bike blasted up the road to Coín and some time later Wilson returned to the bar, pulling out a 9mm pistol and shooting Smith twice in the crowded pub as he attempted to get up from his seat. Eleven times the furious Wilson pulled the trigger as shocked revellers looked on. Less than 48 hours after the attack he was arrested at his farm, where Spanish police found explosives, grenades and fake passports. Searching his rented home, officers also found electronic detonators and cylinders filled with explosives in a bedside chest of drawers. After years of murder the writing was on the wall for the Wilsons. In 2011 Keith Wilson, then 23, was sentenced to life in prison for the shooting of 25-year-old Daniel Gaynor. That same year 'Lucky' was handed down 23 years for the murder of Smith, and one year later John Wilson was gunned down in front of his seven-year-old daughter, leaving just Alan and young Luke under the management of Hunt.

In Spain the Kinahan mob were ramping up their own activities and Daniel Kinahan decided he had a new job opportunity: an in-house killer who would work for him full time and be paid a bonus every time his services as an assassin were required. The expansion of the Kinahan network was about growing but also about keeping business decisions within a tight-knit and trusted team. Kinahan found that there were plenty of takers from his own inner circle of childhood friends and those of his closest associates when it came to making a living from a gun. Among the boxing enthusiasts and street fighters he'd surrounded himself with was James Quinn, a skilled fighter who had been blooded by his uncle Martin 'The Viper' Foley, who'd often brought him to off-grid bare-knuckle bouts in the mountains outside Dublin when he was growing up. Quinn had been reared in the Oliver Bond flat complex where the Kinahan boys, Daniel and Christopher Jr, lived with their mother, Jean Boylan, a cleaning lady. Quinn was very close to Boylan, who'd regularly fed him as a child and shown him kindness. He kept a dog-eared picture of her in his wallet and referred to her as his 'surrogate ma'. Quinn had amassed a string of convictions for violent assaults and regularly threatened bouncers and gardaí after getting into incidents in pubs in the city, but he was looking for a chance to get out of Dublin and live the expensive Costa lifestyle that the Kinahans were enjoying. His temper meant he wasn't an ideal candidate for the business end of the drugs business, which required a degree of self-control. At one point in 2008 Quinn was so incapable of managing his emotions that he'd warned a doorman he'd be sorry for putting him out of a pub and returned later with a hammer and smashed the windscreen of a Garda car. Around the early 2010s Quinn had started spending more and more time in Spain, where he worked as a driver for Kinahan and where he finally found his role in the mob, kept on a retainer to kill. The Kinahan cartel were a very structured grouping, with pay rates for everything from transport to murder, and they had at least two other Dubliners operating as hitmen and working on a bonus scheme. Both had young families and wives and somehow managed to compartmentalise their work from their seemingly ordinary existence, but Quinn threw himself into the life of a high-flying gangster, living on a yacht and flashing his cash on drugs, fast cars, high-end watches and women.

While gang leaders and drug wholesalers had no moral problem with ordering a killing, few did the dirty work themselves, largely because of the mandatory life sentence that awaited them should they be caught. Unlike the never-ending stream of youngsters willing to stand on a street corner as a lookout, or hold or transport drugs, killers were a more finite group. Gang leaders with ambition needed trusted hitmen, so they tended to favour killers from within their own inner circle. In Coolock a rising star in gangland had, like Daniel Kinahan, employed from within his tight group of childhood friends. The mobster known as Mr Big was a powerful force and his secret weapon was the killer Kenneth Finn, in whom he had total trust and who was a loyal servant when it came to the business of crime. Finn was a debt collector for Mr Big, a master at armed robbery and tiger kidnapping while still in his 20s. Tiger kidnapping is the abduction, usually from an institution such as a bank, of a high-value individual who is then kept as ransom until demands for money are met. Just like Marlo Hyland, Mr Big was using the profits to invest in drug wholesaling, which was making him very rich and powerful. He had a fearsome reputation on the estates where he'd grown up and with Finn at his side he was fast gaining a reputation as one not to cross.

When Minister Michael McDowell told his Cabinet colleagues at a briefing in 2006 that there was to be a major crackdown on suspected members of drug gangs across Dublin city, he insisted that there was no 'Mr Big'. However, Big's outfit were the chief suspects for the murder that sparked the operation, that of 22-year-old father of one James Purdue, the sixth murder in the north Dublin area in a matter of months and the 29th that year. Purdue had been gunned down as he returned to his apartment in Donaghmede. Just two weeks earlier Keith Fitzsimons, 23, had been shot dead as he stood in his garden in a case of mistaken identity. Both were accused of owing money to Big and his pals. Like most gang bosses, Mr Big was ambitious. He had come up through armed robbery and tiger kidnapping in a traditional route to drug supply that had taught him valuable lessons in how to outfox the Gardaí, remain alert at all times and leave nothing to chance. He'd formed part of a large grouping from Coolock that had worked in the dust of the likes of Micka 'The Panda' Kelly and his pal Paul 'Burger' Walsh, along with Sean Dunne. Dunne was a fraudster and dealer who'd used a complex VAT scam to raise money to buy large consignments of drugs, turning him into a multi-millionaire property owner in both Ireland and Spain before he vanished without trace on the Costa Blanca. Mr Big had a clear vision for himself as a leader and not an underling, and he had the sense to respect those above him, not go to war unnecessarily and to wait for opportunities rather than rush in. He had very carefully built up contacts north as well as south of the border and was deeply embedded in his own community of Coolock, where he had grown up.

McDowell's promise of changes to legislation and more Garda recruitment sounded exciting and positive for those fighting organised crime from swish offices and at fancy desks, but on the ground, officers on the beat had noticed an ever-more violent situation developing throughout the noughties as the demand for cocaine soared and the economy boomed. There had always been headbangers involved in organised crime, but it seemed a new breed of thugs, fuelled by their own cocaine supply, were becoming far more trigger-happy when it came to solving a dispute or even finishing an argument. Most of them were coming of age and being spat out of those massive social housing estates built as a beacon of hope by long-retired politicians and power brokers for a new generation.

Robbie Lawlor was exactly the type of new-breed gangster that 1980s drug kingpin Larry Dunne had warned the court about when he was finally sent down. Born in 1985, Lawlor had grown up in Foxhill in Coolock on Dublin's northside. Although he came from a close-knit family, with two sisters and a brother, by the time he was a young teenager Lawlor was out of control, unpredictable and known to the Gardaí as being involved in car thefts and small-time drug dealing. The family had moved into the area as part of the slum clearance of the north inner city. His mother Celia's second relationship was with a taxi driver, Paul Dillon, and she changed her name when she remarried. Lawlor was a classic teen soldier for the gangs around the area. He was known as a loose cannon; happy and good fun one minute and ferocious and dangerous the next. He dropped out of school unable to deal with its authoritarian structure and, quick to take offence, fell out with childhood friends. Those who knew him knew to walk on eggshells around him and avoid stoking that hot temper that was always bubbling to the surface. It was that reckless approach to the world and his total unpredictability that would go on to make him an indiscriminate killer motivated by both money and personal grievances. Lawlor was a vain sort, too, spending a lot of time honing his physique in the gym. He was a ladies' man, but teenage sweetheart Rachel Kirwan was his number one girl and he charmed and terrorised her in equal measures. At 17 he was before the courts for dealing drugs and quickly racked up three more convictions for possession, road traffic offences and charges relating to stolen vehicles. By 19 his quick temper had got him a name in Garda circles as one to approach with caution. He was brought to Swords District Court that year after giving a false name and address when stopped and the judge was told he had been so violent that it had taken three officers to restrain him.

On that occasion he was fined, but he spent the next few years in and out of prison and would ultimately amass more than 124 convictions during his life of crime. His first murder would tell gardaí a lot about the individual who would go on to become an enemy of the State, largely because of the motive, the planning and the execution.

Mark Byrne was 31 and serving a sentence for robbery when in May 2005 he was granted temporary release on compassionate grounds because of a family issue. Byrne had pedigree as a criminal. He was from Kilcarrig Green in Tallaght and had served time in Portlaoise, where he had befriended the notorious John Gilligan. At one point he had escaped custody while on a hospital visit and he was well able to handle himself in the rough and tumble of life behind bars. Like Lawlor, he was hot-headed, and the two had clashed at Wheatfield Prison, where they were both serving time; the older man had overpowered Lawlor and believed he had put him in his place. Byrne had no clue just how long Lawlor could hold a grudge or, indeed, how well connected he was within the prison system, even at the tender age of 20. When Byrne was granted his temporary release he had no idea that fellow lags were using smuggled mobile phones to stay in touch with Lawlor, who had made it known he was happy to pay for any information he could get on Byrne and his movements. At 10am on 4 May 2005, the door of Mountjoy Training Unit opened and Byrne strolled out into the late spring sun. He walked a few hundred metres to a newsagent on the junction of Vincent Street and Berkeley Road, where he bought credit for his mobile phone. As he walked out of the shop he was approached from behind and shot at point-blank range as commuters and shoppers looked on in terror. Witnesses would later tell gardaí investigating the murder about a cool, calm and ruthless killer who escaped on foot. They described seeing the man, wearing dark clothing, a hoodie and a baseball cap, approach Byrne from behind as he was preoccupied with his phone. Officers were told that witnesses heard firing and saw him fall to the ground; he tried to scramble away on his hands and knees, but the hooded man stood over him and shot again. Such was the force of the impact of that bullet that it flipped him over. The gunman calmly leaned down to check his victim was dead before running away.

The execution of such a hardened criminal shocked gardaí, who knew immediately that Lawlor, who had been released from prison just months earlier, was their chief suspect. A joint investigation got under way both inside and outside the prison, with 112 witness statements taken. Lawlor was arrested and questioned but, like a veteran, he refused to co-operate or answer any questions that officers had for him. The murder was the fifth gangland killing of the year and placed the focus on smuggled phones in prisons and what they were being used for.

Months after Byrne's murder a criminal trial was told that the killing of Paul Warren, 24, on a night in February the year before had been directly co-ordinated by a prisoner using a smuggled phone. Warren was drinking at a bar in Grays pub at Newmarket Square off Cork Street when two masked and armed men burst into the premises shortly before closing time. One of the men shot at him in front of terrified customers as he fled to the toilets for safety. He was gunned down before he could find shelter from the bullets. Warren was a suspect in the murder of Joey Rattigan, carried out by the hitman Paddy Doyle. Rattigan's brother Brian was then serving a prison sentence but officers believed he had ordered and directed Warren's assassination from behind bars. The hit on Warren was carried out by John Roche, who would in turn be shot dead within a year. Mobile phones had for years been thrown over the perimeter walls of the jail to prisoners in the exercise yards, but netting had put paid to that. Authorities now feared that newer and smaller phones were entering the jails concealed internally by criminals on committal or by those returning after periods of temporary release. Once smuggled in they were being concealed in cells, in the U-bends of toilets and down drain holes and they were being used to facilitate the arrangement of murders and drug deals. In the aftermath of Byrne's murder, new camera technology was being tested, including guided lenses that could be placed down water pipes and other hard-to-search areas.

Weeks after Robbie Lawlor killed his first victim, Justice Minister Michael McDowell claimed that gangland crime was dissipating and those involved in the activity were 'on the back foot'. He also promised that Operation Anvil would strike at the heart of Dublin's gun culture. The new operation, he explained, gave the Gardaí an extra 15,000 hours overtime per week to investigate gang leaders who had ordered a spate of killings and armed robberies. A budget of €6.5 million had been set aside to 'strike at the heart' of Dublin's growing gun culture. Despite their efforts, gardaí could not find enough to charge Lawlor; three years after Byrne's murder, in 2008, a coroner's court would hear that the Director of Public Prosecutions had ruled that there was not enough evidence against the identified shooter. Coroner Dr Brian Farrell described the murder as a particularly cruel shooting and 'obviously a targeted one'.

While Lawlor wasn't named at the inquest, he was during a Dublin District Court hearing in October of that year, when it was disclosed that Lawlor, who was then 22 years old, had been arrested as a suspect in the shooting of another man, Anthony Ayodeji, in Darndale the previous July and that his girlfriend Rachel Kirwan, 24, had been quizzed about withholding information. The attempt to kill Ayodeji had been a truly shocking gun attack that had sparked a political outcry in a country that had seen a decade of bloody gang wars between rival gangs in Crumlin in Dublin and in Limerick, where the McCarthy–Dundon gang had gone to war with the rival Keane–Collopy outfit. Ayodeji had been holding a baby boy and sitting in a car when he was blasted with five shots through a window of the Volkswagen Golf. The baby was covered in blood and glass but miraculously escaped death and serious injury. Ayodeji took three bullets and was rushed to hospital in critical condition. Witnesses said they had seen a masked gunman walk calmly up Buttercup Park in Darndale towards the car before raising his weapon. The car had been parked near a green area surrounded by houses and while people rushed out when they heard the gunshots, the would-be killer had made his getaway. Lawlor had been arrested and questioned about the shooting of Ayodeji, who was of Lebanese origin and who had been minding the 22-month-old son of a female friend at the time of the shooting. But, again, officers didn't have enough to charge him with the crime. In the case of

Ayodeji, the motive again appeared to be a personal grievance. Months after the shooting, Rachel Kirwan, Lawlor's girlfriend, had launched a court bid to have her car returned to her, resulting in the pair being named before the court as suspects in the crime. Their Volkswagen Passat had been seized by gardaí investigating that shooting as they believed it had been used to carry Lawlor to and from the scene. Kirwan had brought the police property application to Dublin District Court but gardaí had resisted it, insisting the car was still a key piece of evidence. Over the course of the case it was heard that Kirwan had been arrested on suspicion of withholding information from gardaí, while Lawlor was a suspect in the shooting. The court heard that gardaí had been informed by lawyers for both Kirwan and Lawlor that neither needed the vehicle to be forensically examined and she had sent three letters looking for the car back. In evidence lawyers said she was paying €500 a month for the car, which she couldn't use as it had been three and a half months in possession of the Gardaí and that she was under 'considerable pressure'.

In March 2009 Lawlor claimed his next victim. David 'Fred' Lynch was shot three times in the head with a semi-automatic pistol and his body dumped on wasteland. The murder showed gardaí that Lawlor was not only a ruthless killer but also a treacherous one – he was willing to take on and take out just about anyone. Lynch, a low-level thug known as 'Fred', was the father of a young boy. He was also a friend of Lawlor's, but he was involved in disputes with a large number of criminals in the Coolock area which had upped the murder rate in the district to staggering levels. His was the 12th gangland killing of that year. He'd left his mother's house on the afternoon of 29 March, telling her, 'I'll be back in ten minutes, I'm going to meet Robbie Lawlor.' The purpose of the meeting with Lawlor and another associate, Noel Deans, was to dig up a gun on waste ground in Belcamp. When they retrieved the weapon, Lawlor had shot Lynch without warning. More than a year later, another close friend of Lawlor, Mr Big's hitman Kenneth Finn, was drinking with Deans in the Priorswood Inn in Coolock. Deans was drunk and was openly bragging that he had been with Lawlor when he shot Lynch. Finn phoned Lawlor and told him what Deans was saying. When the pair left the pub at 10pm they turned into a pedestrian lane, where Lawlor was waiting. He shot Deans in the head and body. Deans had been a classic chaotic young criminal who was aged just 27 when he died. He had spent most of his life in child detention centres and adult prisons and was known as a disorganised criminal who was anti-establishment and up for any crime that would fund his drug habit. In 2000, aged 18, he was jailed for four years for using a stolen car to ram a Garda vehicle and then reverse over an officer on foot. His trial heard he had begun smoking cannabis at 13 years of age before moving on to harder drugs like heroin and crack cocaine. At a later trial for another altercation with a Garda car and for attacking an officer, a judge was told that he was first jailed at 14 and over the preceding seven years had been just 18 months out of custody. The court was also told he had psychiatric problems and a drug addiction. The murder of Deans was inevitable and nobody would avenge his death, but it certainly cemented Lawlor's reputation as a cool and calculated killer.

As Lawlor lurched in and out of feuding gangs, spent regular stints behind bars and made it known that he was a gun for hire, a far more organised killer was about to make a name for himself on Dublin's northside. Despite their claims to be ridding the capital of drug dealers, in reality the Dublin branch of the Real IRA, under the leadership of the suave womaniser Alan Ryan, were putting the heavy on dealers and criminals, intimidating them and extorting money from them. Ryan had been ambitious since taking charge of the dissident group and had gone for the big players as well as the small, quickly becoming a cause of concern for some Real IRA bosses in the North who were worried that he'd become too powerful and a potential liability. His extortion rackets were worth hundreds of thousands of euros. Ryan, originally from Grange Abbey Drive in Donaghmede, was a skilled gunman and had first been jailed at 19 for attending a Real IRA training camp. It was in 1999 when Ryan was caught along with older dissidents at Stamullen in County Meath and while he awaited trial he was caught with a gun. The training camp had been targeted by the Garda's Special Detective Unit designated to police dissident activity across the country. They watched as ten men gathered at a farm and gardaí discovered assault rifles, a submachine gun and a semi-automatic pistol in a cellar. Ryan received four years for his role in the camp and a separate three years on firearms charges. He quickly gained respect from dissidents while serving his sentences in Portlaoise.

When he was released from jail Ryan decided to go to war with the drug gangs who were flooding the country with their product and making huge money. He demanded large sums of cash off them and if they refused to pay up they became targets for his feared dissident gang, who traded under the IRA name. Ryan had made plenty of enemies during his campaigns of extortion against the criminal gangs. Ryan became involved in a bitter dispute with Sean 'The Smuggler' Hunt when he turned to him for money and the Ballyfermot criminal refused. As part of the dispute the Real IRA were believed to have shot Colm 'Collie' Owens, an associate of Hunt. Owens was shot at his workplace, the Corn Store animal feed warehouse at the Grove Industrial Estate in Finglas. Owens was best known for being an associate of Eamon 'The Don' Dunne, the ruthless criminal who had taken over the 'Marlo' Hyland firm after the boss was killed. The shooting of Owens was casual. It had happened at midday and witnesses said the gunman had walked up to Owens and shot him up to eight times at close range in front of several other employees. After the shooting the gunman had escaped in a waiting silver Audi A4 car, which had driven in the direction of Finglas, colliding with two other cars at the Tolka Valley Road junction, before being abandoned and burnt out.

In a revenge attack Hunt had enlisted Alan, Keith and John Wilson to murder Ryan at the Player's Lounge pub in Fairview, where he was a regular. The operation was a catastrophe. Instead of targeting Ryan, Alan Wilson had managed to shoot three innocent men, including the pub doorman, in a spray of bullets. The shooting attempt was like nothing gardaí had seen before and was later described as a narco-style drive-by shooting akin to Mafia assassinations of the 1930s. CCTV showed a gunman opening fire with a fully loaded semi-automatic pistol, randomly spraying 9mm rounds at the pub and then making his getaway in a Volkswagen Golf, which was later torched.

Ryan was incensed but not scared, and rather than backing off he stepped up his activities and was believed to have killed drug dealer Sean Winters, who was shot twice in the head outside an apartment in Portmarnock in September 2010, in the immediate aftermath.

A year later, Ryan would claim a far bigger player in an effort to rubber stamp his ability to extort from the big hitters of the underworld, but the murder of Michael 'The Panda' Kelly would ultimately leave a clear path of progress for his underlings in the Mr Big network. Kelly, originally from the Kilbarrack area, was regarded as the biggest player on Dublin's northside when he was hit up by Ryan and his cohorts for money, but he resisted handing over any of his spoils. The Panda was just 30 years old but had risen through the ranks of the underworld by murdering rivals who had got in his way. He had a close relationship with the then heir to the Irish mafia, Daniel Kinahan, and was one of the few Dublin kingpins who was regularly seen in his company in Spain. He'd been a target of CAB, which had relieved him of a house in County Meath and two expensive cars. In an effort to mark their power, Ryan's Real IRA demanded a cut of his profits, but were laughed at. As a result they killed him on the street outside the home he shared with new mum Caoimhe Robinson. The daylight killing of Kelly at his home in Clongriffin would not only remove one of the most bloodthirsty criminals from the gangland scene, but it would clear a path for Mr Big to take over the vast north Dublin turf Kelly had controlled.

Kelly, who was originally from Kilbarrack, earned his money through massive shipments of cocaine. Despite his strong connections with the Kinahan mob, he had his own suppliers too. Over the course of his career he'd ordered at least six murders, the first being an entirely innocent man, 23-year-old Keith Fitzsimons, who'd been killed in a case of mistaken identity near his home in Kilbarrack. Two years later he had rival Anto Russell shot dead in a pub in Artane and three months after that Anthony Foster was gunned down at his home in Coolock. At the same time he'd employed Eric 'Lucky' Wilson to help him settle his differences with the drug dealers David 'Babyface' Lindsay and Alan Napper, who'd been lured to a rural property, killed, dismembered and disappeared. The Panda had terrorised local dealers in the wider Coolock neighbourhoods and ruled with an iron fist. After his death the Real IRA claimed the murder, spray-painting 'RIRA anti drugs. Micka Kelly drug dealer dead,' on a wall in their northside stronghold. Within one month of his death the PSNI had shut down the double murder investigation into the disappearance of Lindsay and Napper in 2008.

Ryan felt empowered by the brazen take-out of such a big player on the drug scene and he immediately turned his attentions to the veteran criminal Eamon Kelly, a mentor and elder to many gangsters and the go-between for Dublin gangs with Christy 'The Dapper Don' Kinahan, father of Daniel and by then the biggest wholesaler in Europe. It was during late 2011 and the first half of 2012 that tit-for-tat arguments with Mr Big also intensified and at one point Ryan's mob stole a large amount of money from the Big organisation. Mr Big had been busy raising funds so he could invest in larger drug shipments and had carried out a number of high-netting robberies, one of which involved the kidnap of a family over a lengthy period. In his mind, Mr Big had earned his money and was not going to hand it over to anyone. The simple solution to the problem that Ryan had become was to shoot him, but criminals worried about what would follow the assassination of such a high-profile dissident figure. For decades there had been a largely respectful relationship between the criminals and the terrorists who conducted their activities on an island divided by a border and where, despite ceasefires and gun amnesties, an arsenal of gunpower still existed in the North. OCGs had long preferred to keep the Provos and, later, groups like the Continuity IRA and the Real IRA happy, either through tithes or diplomatic sharing of resources. They also asked for permission if they wanted to interfere with any of their 'volunteers'. But Ryan had shifted the balance and the intensity of his demands had made him a lot of enemies with connections deep in the Northern dissident groups, where suspicions about him remained even within his own Northern command. In a show of his own growing power base in north Dublin, Mr Big stepped up to negotiate a plan. When it had been sanctioned by the Kinahans in Spain, he made his move.

At 3.30 on the afternoon of 3 September 2012, Ryan, then 32, was shot at Grange Lodge Avenue in Clongriffin as he walked along the street towards his home. It was the place he felt safest and could never conceive that he'd be targeted there. As he collapsed on the ground, Mr Big's hitman, Kenneth Finn, walked over and shot him in the head before escaping in a car which was later found burnt out in a graveyard. The murder was a bold move. It was the first time the criminals had put it up to the ruthless dissidents in such a high-profile way. For months expectations grew that the wider Northern command of the Real IRA would take bloody retribution for Ryan's death. Instead, little followed save the assassination of the elderly criminal Eamon Kelly as he walked home from a bookies' office. The 65-year-old had escaped an attempt on his life but believed he was safe with Ryan out of the picture. The daring murder of Ryan caused chaos within his own ranks and resulted in the merging of groups into a new movement called the New IRA, which was intent on cleaning up its image and restructuring into a disciplined force. The group included Real IRA, Republican Action Against Drugs (RAAD) and Óglaigh na hÉireann members, along with a hardcore group of veteran Provos who'd previously sat on the sidelines. While they did come out in force to mourn Ryan, with a full colour party and shots fired over his grave, the reality was that the murdered dissident had been on a crash course with his own leadership for a long time, thanks to the intensity of his operations in Dublin and the levels of publicity that had followed. While dissident groupings publicly claimed Ryan as a hero, behind the scenes they had long had concerns about his high-profile activities and many believed that had he not been taken out by Mr Big, he would have fallen foul of his own. Within weeks the New IRA were interrogating his closest associates, and pals Nathan Kinsella and Declan Smith were quizzed and then shot in the legs under accusations that money that had been paid to the group had not made it to the war chest in the North. As the group looked inwards they killed one of their own, Peter Butterly, who was shot dead outside the Huntsman Inn in Gormanstown, Meath in March 2013 as students waiting for their school bus looked on.

One year later, with the movement still in chaos and its members under the close watch of the Special Detective Unit, Mr Big saw another opportunity, this time targeting Ryan's right-hand man, Deccie Smith. The 32-year-old died a week after being shot in the face as he dropped his son off at a crèche. Originally from the Cliftonville Road in north Belfast, he'd been living in the Republic since 2007. Smith was vulnerable because he faced the twin threat of Mr Big and the dissidents. He couldn't go back to the North because he was wanted there for questioning by the PSNI as a suspect in the murders of Edward Burns, 36, and Joe Jones, 38, both members of the Continuity IRA, who'd been beaten and killed in a row over money and missing weapons. But he'd made a schoolboy error when he decided to move to Coolock in an effort to hide in the vastness of its housing estates. By doing so he had placed himself in the heartland of Mr Big's territory and given him the opportunity to watch his regular movements and come up with a plan. The entire scenario brought fame to Mr Big in criminal circles, respect to his hitman Finn and new opportunities for him to grow as a force to be reckoned with.

While the Big network grew in the Coolock area, fighting its way to power, Robbie Lawlor would have been an obvious choice of hitman for hire, but there were family reasons for not aligning with his one-time neighbour. Lawlor had continued to move in and out of the prison system, to grow his reputation as a hardened killer and enforcer. His relationship with Rachel

Kirwan remained volatile and at one point in December 2014 he was arrested and later charged with assault causing harm to her at her home in Grangemore Crescent in Donaghmede. When he was caught a year later with a stolen car he was handed down a hefty 16-month sentence due to how familiar his face had become in the dock of a courtroom.

But while Lawlor's life was chaotic, the same could not be said for his brother-in-law Richie Carberry, who had risen to become a serious player on the organised crime scene. Once a member of the same crew that Mr Big had worked in, he decided that he wanted to go it alone and operate independently from the gang now under the leadership of his former contemporary. Originally from Riversdale Drive in Coolock, Carberry wasn't into the dirty business of getting hands-on with his drug supply or with the murkier business of the world he lived in. He preferred to see himself as a boss and liked to remain below the radar as he muscled in on drugs turf and eyed up opportunities in the market. Married to Eileen, Lawlor's eldest sister, he had become a father in 2003 when he was just in his early 20s. Five years older than his brother-in-law, he was organising shipments, laundering money and building up a fortune for himself and his growing family throughout his 20s. A year after the birth of his first child, a daughter, he registered a business name, C.MAC Construction, from his Coolock address, with a co-owner, but it ceased operating within a year. By 2007 he'd registered his address in a more upmarket home at Castlemartin Drive in Bettystown, County Meath. He'd changed his occupation too and was now the owner of RC Interiors.

The move to Bettystown and the residential estate on the edge of the village was an opportunity for Carberry to live below the radar of police and away from the neighbourhoods where the notorious Mr Big was becoming a force to be reckoned with. Bettystown had long been a holiday destination for north Dubliners before the Algarve or the Costa del Sol became an affordable reality. While it had once been a small country village, the growing population of Dublin and the knockout property prices of the Celtic Tiger had turned it into a bustling commuter town. Seaside cottages had made way for large housing estates and apartment complexes, and coffee shops and big supermarkets had sprung up to cater for the growing population. Carberry's business partner had moved to the County Meath countryside too and together they set about protecting their corner of the cocaine market in Dublin. Carberry prided himself on being a family man and providing for his brood of three children, Codie, Charlie and Callum, who had been born in quick succession. He doted on Eileen, lavishing her with gifts and holidays, and while neighbours believed the couple were simply successful business people, he feathered their nest with the proceeds of his lucrative drug trade. But Carberry's ambition was not satisfied with a big new home, a flash car or the façade of being upwardly mobile; he wanted more, and the nearby town of Drogheda and its burgeoning population of commuters caught his eye. By 2016 the census showed that the population of Bettystown, nearby Laytown and Mornington had doubled in the years since the new millennium and that was before the surge of homeowners in the bigger town of Drogheda, located just a 15-minute drive from

Bettystown. The area ticked many boxes for workers, including a regular direct train service to Connolly Station in the heart of the capital. Drogheda's population had swelled because of property refugees from Dublin who were simply priced out of the housing market there. The census showed that between them Bettystown, Laytown and Mornington had a population of around 34,000 while Drogheda by then housed over 44,000 people. The nearby Fingal constituencies of Balbriggan and Swords had combined populations of more than 125,000, making the whole area rival Waterford, Galway and Limerick in terms of population. Surveys estimated that around 20,000 people left Drogheda every day to travel to work, a young and wealthy cohort who mainly came back to their commuter towns to socialise . . . and to take cocaine.

CHAPTER THREE

An Opportunity to Kill

The gunmen who stormed the Regency Hotel disguised as members of the Garda Síochána failed in their attempt to kill the head of the Kinahan Cartel, Daniel Kinahan, during a boxing weigh-in. But they had created the climate for all-out war in the underworld. While the hit team had missed Kinahan after he slipped out the back of the hotel, they had assassinated his underling David Byrne in reception, lighting the flames of a deadly feud between two of Ireland's biggest gangland mobs – the Kinahan and the Hutch organisations. Once a united force, the rival groupings knew everything about one another, meaning that no time would be wasted gathering intelligence around potential targets. Revenge had been swift in a city locked down by the Gardaí, who feared the worst; just three days after Kinahan escaped with his life, Eddie Hutch, the oldest brother of the infamous Gerry 'The Monk' Hutch, was brutally shot dead at the door of his home.

It had all started in a row over money in the Kinahans' adopted homeland of the Costa del Sol. The friendship between Gary Hutch, a nephew of The Monk, and Daniel Kinahan, heir to an eye-watering drug fortune, had once been so tight that friends joked of a 'bromance'. But when things soured through a mix of jealousy and paranoia, the feud had carried over to Dublin, where the two sides lined up against one another and where the Lanzarote-based head of the Hutch family, Gerry 'The Monk' Hutch, was drawn out of retirement in an effort to broker peace. In the aftermath of the Regency and the murder of Eddie Hutch, the first of four family members who would be assassinated during the feud, the capital was on a knife edge, with the potential for mass murder by the wealthy Kinahan organisation in no doubt. In the glare of publicity that had followed the Regency outrage, captured on videos taken on mobile phones and reported across the world as a 'narco spectacular', Minister for Justice Frances Fitzgerald had allocated an extra €5 million for 'saturation policing' to try to secure the north inner-city area where the Hutch gang and many innocent family members lived in what was described as an 'unprecedented gangland threat'. With two people killed in four days, two major criminal factions at war and a general election under way, the murders of Byrne and Hutch had placed law and order at the very top of the national agenda.

In the Dáil, political enemies were circling too. Sinn Féin's untimely calls to abolish the Special Criminal Court and the then party leader Gerry Adams's announcement shortly before the attack that there was no gangland gave fuel to the opposition and allowed Fianna Fáil's Justice spokesman Niall Collins to denounce the party as a 'cult'. Garda Commissioner Noírín O'Sullivan stood on shaky ground, too, as questions were asked about why members of the media had been in attendance at the boxing weigh-in at the hotel where the brazen shooting had occurred, while the gardaí were not. Minister Fitzgerald had been forced to express her confidence in the police chief, but to add to the chaos, crime journalists had been issued with threat to life notices as the gangs focused their hatred on the media for the first time since the murder of journalist Veronica Guerin more than twenty years before. On the streets, armed checkpoints surrounded the north inner city, rapid response units lay in wait for the next assassination attempt and, covertly, all eyes and ears of the force were on the vast and powerful Kinahan gang, with at least forty members under full-time surveillance and others subject to search and arrest policies. And it was at that moment, with specialist Garda units stretched to their limits across the capital, that the criminal known as Mr Big saw his opportunity for a hat-trick.

On 29 February 2016, Vinny Ryan, the 25-year-old brother of murdered Real IRA head Alan was going about his business having spent the morning with his partner Kelly Smyth at his home in Donaghmede. The couple had celebrated the birth of their daughter just five weeks earlier. Later in the day they decided to go to Smyth's house at McKee Road in Finglas and strapped their newborn into Ryan's white Volkswagen Golf GTI. When they arrived, Smyth got out with the baby and asked Ryan to move the car because it was parked on the grass. When she was inside the house she heard five loud bangs and ran outside with her brother Keith to find the windows of the car smashed and

Ryan fatally injured. In the distance they saw what looked like another Volkswagen Golf speeding away. Vinny, who moonlighted as a barber, had been part of his older brother's dissident army of enforcers who'd taken on drug dealers and demanded a slice of their profits. He'd been arrested after Michael 'Micka' Kelly was shot dead and had faced charges for carrying a firearm on the day he was killed, but he'd been acquitted by a court. Three years since his release from jail and four years since Alan's death he'd been regularly warned that his life was under threat, but he'd insisted that he wanted to avenge the murder of his brother and get even with Mr Big. A number of attempts had been made on his life and he'd even been stabbed as a warning to back down, but he'd continued to refuse to meet with the gang boss to discuss their differences. The daylight hit was brave and bold but carried the trademark opportunism of the man who'd ordered it and of the skill of his hitman, Kenneth Finn, who'd carried it out. The murder in the midst of the chaos following the Regency gave Gardaí a glimpse of an ambition and cunning that set Mr Big apart from his contemporaries and it also proved how he was manoeuvring himself to become a leading criminal force on the island of Ireland.

Mr Big had already proved himself a ruthless player in the underworld as he'd come up the ranks through armed robberies, tiger kidnappings and also as a cocaine and weapons dealer who was determined to run his rivals off his turf. Once an underling, he'd become a boss directing a network of killers in his ranks, including two brothers nicknamed the Taliban. He'd ordered the deaths of small-time criminals who owed him money, perceived rivals who might have tried to take him on and even his own men who'd served their purpose. He had everything it took to make it to the very top of the gangland ladder and he was determined to stay there. Mr Big had a brain for both business and the complexities of murder. He was patient, methodical and calculated, always waiting for the right moment to strike, often when others were looking the other way or when internal rows had taken precedence over external enemies. Undoubtedly he'd made some mistakes, but he'd been lucky in his career and regularly slipped out of the reach of the gardaí who were relentlessly pursuing him. He'd lost a few men along the way into the prison system, but months after his gunman killed Vinny Ryan he was comforted to realise that he was going to get away with one of the biggest errors of his career.

That September a coroner's court heard that the murderer of two innocent cousins brutally killed at a petrol station were unlikely ever to be brought to justice. Mark Noonan was 23 and his cousin Glen Murphy just 19 when they were shot dead on the forecourt of a Tesco filling station in Dublin in 2010. But as their inquest opened, the Dublin Coroner's Court heard that six years on, no file had been submitted to the Director of Public Prosecutions and it was unlikely that it ever would. Mr Big had been the suspect from the beginning and gardaí were sure that it was on his orders that the shooting had happened, but they simply couldn't get enough evidence to solve the case. Apart from luck, there was also safety in the number of gangland cold cases on the books of An Garda Síochána. At that point more than 240 gangland murders had yet to be solved in Ireland and Detective

Inspector Colm Murphy of Finglas Garda Station told the coroner that despite extensive investigations into the double murder, it was unlikely to ever reach a courtroom. The murder was hugely high-profile both because of where it happened and because the killers had got the wrong men. The cousins had pulled into the petrol station to buy cigarettes and sweets, followed by Mr Big's gang, who had used a tracking device attached to the wrong car. The botched hit was meant for rival dealers. Despite heavy Garda resources being devoted to the investigation, detectives couldn't get to Mr Big. The gunmen had fled over the border in the aftermath and notwithstanding high-profile appeals on RTÉ's *Crimecall*, no witnesses had come forward and no evidence of value had been gathered.

Mr Big's hitmen had also been linked to another brutal double murder. Small-time criminals Anthony Burnett and Joseph Redmond were hapless car thieves accused of owing a debt. The duo knew their lives were at risk when they tried to sell a stolen car in March 2012 but they were desperate for cash and had travelled to meet a potential buyer in the hope of pocketing €700. Their murders were uncovered when emergency services were called out to reports that there was a burning car in a layby at Ravensdale Forest Park in County Louth. There, firefighters spotted skulls and ribcages in the burnt-out wreck and later medics identified the duo through DNA swabs taken from their mothers. Post-mortems carried out on the charred remains found that the cause of death in both cases was gunshot wounds to the head. The assassinated pair were low-level criminals from Ballybough involved in the theft of cars for gangsters, and detectives discovered that they were terrified of Mr Big but wanted a few hundred quid so they could celebrate a birthday. They had been called to travel to the North by a potential buyer who'd later be identified as Dublin criminal Jason O'Driscoll, but the whole thing turned out to be a double-cross devised by Mr Big. O'Driscoll had worked for Freddie Thompson and the Kinahan network and would regularly source cars for whatever job he had on, but when he and another associate of Mr Big were snapped in a CCTV image in Armagh shortly after the murders he became wanted for murder. O'Driscoll lay low in Northern Ireland and regularly travelled to Spain after the murders, but officers issued an arrest warrant for him and he was later extradited from Alicante and convicted of the killings.

The underworld knew that Mr Big's own man Paul Gallagher, suspected of being the getaway driver on the Alan Ryan hit, had signed his own death warrant when he fell out with his boss. He'd moved out of the Coolock area for his own safety but regularly came home to visit his family. His mother Geraldine would later tell his inquest that on the night of her son's murder he had told her he was going to Drogheda to help a friend. She said he left in a car driven by Sean Barrett, who was later convicted of withholding information in relation to the case. Two days later she said Barrett told her that he had left her son in Drogheda after he heard gunshots and ran. Barrett was called to give evidence at the inquest and in his Garda statements had detailed a terrifying night that ended in murder in a field on the Louth–Meath border. Barrett often drove Gallagher to destinations and on the night of his murder they had headed along the M1 until Gallagher asked him to stop the car on a hard shoulder and two men got in, one with a crowbar. He told the inquest he didn't know who the men were. In his statements he said they drove to a road where they had been earlier that day and that Gallagher and the two men got out. He said they walked up a field, over a rusty gate and towards a barnyard. Then, he said, he heard gunshots and ran away. Two days later he rang Gallagher's mother, explained what had happened and brought the dead man's sister and brother to the scene, where the body was discovered. Detective Sergeant Raymond Smith told the inquest that 198 statements had been taken and 150 lines of inquiry followed but, despite the arrest of nine people, no one was ever charged with the murder.

As the body count went up and each murder showed military-style planning, Mr Big's reputation as a terrifying force in the underworld grew. He had maintained a friendly relationship with Daniel Kinahan in Spain and often purchased cartel products while also developing his own independent network of suppliers in Europe and beyond. His own relationship had brought the pair into far more intimate contact. Kinahan had begun dating Caoimhe Robinson, the widow of murdered Michael 'Micka' Kelly. Despite his rivalry with Kelly, Mr Big's own partner was one of Robinson's best pals and the couple had spent a lot of time in Kinahan's company as a result, regularly visiting Spain, where he mixed business and pleasure with the head of the powerful cartel. Robinson was a pretty blonde who had witnessed the full horrors of gangland when she saw Kelly murdered, but that hadn't turned her off a relationship with another drug boss. Robinson had been left with little after the death of Kelly, whom she had discovered dying from gunshot wounds on the road outside her home. She had carried their newborn baby in her arms as she followed his coffin to his funeral, but it wasn't long before CAB moved in and picked at the bones of his empire, seizing cars and a house. Robinson had mourned for her loss, then dusted herself down, and was soon back holidaying on the Costa del Sol and secretly dating Kinahan. While Mr Big and Kinahan had trivial and business conversations over meals with their partners, the Coolock boss was careful not to compromise his own interests by getting too drawn into the cartel. As the Dublin underworld burned in the aftermath of the Regency Hotel attack, he let it be known that he was going to stay neutral in the Kinahan and Hutch feud and instead concentrated on mopping up the business opportunities that followed the state crackdown on the two organisations.

From a corporate point of view the feud suited Mr Big. It had been relentless from the beginning. Shortly after the murder of Eddie Hutch, the Kinahan mob struck again when they gunned down The Monk's lifelong pal Noel Duggan outside his home in Ratoath in County Meath. The veteran cigarette smuggler known as Kingsize had nothing to do with the Regency Hotel attack but was targeted because of his friendship with Hutch. A month later an innocent homeless man, Martin O'Rourke, was shot dead in Sheriff Street in Dublin's north inner city in a case of mistaken identity. It is understood a gunman hired by the Kinahan mob had attempted to shoot a Hutch associate but targeted O'Rourke instead. By April 2016, dissident Michael Barr had been shot dead at the Sunset House pub in central Dublin by a gunman wearing a Freddy Krueger mask. Less than a month later Gareth

Hutch, a 35-year-old nephew of The Monk, was murdered by a Kinahan hit squad at the Avondale House complex where he lived. In July David 'Daithi' Douglas was shot dead outside his wife's shoe shop by Kinahan killers and in August an innocent tourist, Trevor O'Neill, was gunned down in Mallorca by a triggerman who tried to kill Gareth Hutch's brother Jonathan, who was holidaying on the island. Before the year's end, The Monk's pal Noel Kirwan, 62, who had attended Eddie Hutch's funeral, was murdered. The killings coming in such quick succession and happening in such public places had led to a sense of unrest and the Gardaí came under huge pressure to regain control. Heavily funded and resourced, they thwarted other attempted murders – The Monk's brothers Johnny and Patsy – hit teams were swept up in high-profile undercover operations and slowly the critical threat level that existed in the north inner city began to abate, but not without the full resources of the State and in particular the Garda's powerful Drugs and Organised Crime Bureau deployed to deal with the emergency situation.

Mr Big knew he was in the right place at the right time, as long as he stayed out of the chaos, and not just because of the amount of resources the Gardaí were drawing on to deal with the feud, but also because he knew that it would destabilise the Kinahans' stranglehold on the Irish drug market and the power it had created. For years the Spanish-based mob had been the biggest supplier of cocaine, cannabis and weapons into Ireland. Such was its success that it was reported that the Kinahans controlled up to 90 per cent of the cocaine flooding the country; that was no exaggeration. For over a decade allegiances to the Kinahan mob had automatically meant protection for any of the sub-cells working for them and an unquestioned authority over other groupings. But as the Garda's multi-pronged operation against them began to take effect, rival outfits had started to challenge that autonomy, creating chaos in areas like Coolock, where Mr Big was headquartered.

Twenty-two-year-old Sean Little had some criminal pedigree, but it was his blood ties with a junior member of the Kinahan organisation that elevated him to a top position in Coolock well before his years and limited experience in the drugs business should have allowed. Little's cousin had been named in court documents as being a member of the wider Kinahan OCG and it was that connection that had made him feel untouchable as he ran his drugs gang in Coolock and spent his money on flash holidays, drivers and designer clothing. Little was closely connected with another young criminal known as 'Mr Flashy', who had been mentored by the Kinahan hitman Trevor Byrne, who had run the mob's cell in Finglas for years. When Byrne was forced to go on the run in the aftermath of a number of feud-related murders, including that of Eddie Hutch, Mr Flashy stepped in to take the top position but quickly angered a number of his contemporaries who didn't want to work for him. Together Little and Mr Flashy had cut a confident swagger as the new bosses, believing themselves to be untouchable under the Kinahan umbrella. But they had misread the room and Little's pal, Zach Parker, became the first to be targeted for attempts to collect drug debts; he was murdered outside a gym in January 2019. Little was furious but still confident that his links to the Kinahan network would terrify those who'd been so daring as to take out one of his men. Social media would form a huge part of the gang war that followed and as tensions rose platforms like Instagram were used to translate threats and show loyalties. At Parker's funeral Little dressed in the uniform of the Kinahan cartel – the same black suit, blue shirt and navy tie worn by hordes of young men who'd attended the funeral of Regency victim David Byrne in 2016, a brazenly Mafia-style event that had struck fear into the nation. Mr Flashy posed for photos with two suspected hitmen at the ceremony, and expensive floral tributes to Parker displayed the logos of Hugo Boss and Louis Vuitton. Little's best friend, Parker was 23 and had trained as a barber. In the underworld he lived in he believed that because of his links to the big players in Spain and Dubai in the United Arab Emirates, when he demanded payment of a debt it would be forthcoming – but instead the bullets pumped into him as he sat in a BMW Jeep outside a gym in Swords marked the first of many coups to be staged by those who no longer believed in the all-encompassing power of the cartel name.

Months after the death of his friend, Little was killed after being lured to a lonely roadside where he was blasted multiple times in the head. His gang hit back, targeting Hamid Sanambar, an odd bod Iranian who'd worked as Little's driver but who they blamed for the double-cross that had led him to the roadside ambush. Sanambar had shown up in Dublin in the company of Kinahan enforcers around 2017, becoming the talk of the underworld for the teardrop gang tattoos on his face. It had been rumoured that he had been trained by Isis and was an expert in beheading and that he had been sent to Dublin by Daniel

Kinahan to finish off some of his rivals who had escaped murder bids. Nothing could have been further from the truth. In fact, he had been in Ireland for years, landing a three-year suspended sentence for a robbery in a brothel in Cork back in 2012.

Sanambar had been seen in a car around the time of the Little murder with 22-year-old drug dealer Eoin Boylan, and that had been enough to seal his fate. Later, when Boylan was accused of gloating about the Little murder in a social media post, he was also targeted and died by shooting six months later after surviving numerous assassination attempts. In the middle of the Little gang massacre another young dealer, Jordan Davis, had been killed because of a separate drug debt he allegedly owed to an out-of-control gangland figure who was waging his own war on perceived enemies. Within a year, five murders had been carried out among a single friendship group of young men in their twenties, though Garda interventions had prevented many more murders. WhatsApp messages were distributed to spread the social media threats and intimidation that accompanied the deaths. One letter sent to the Little family and widely distributed contained the words, 'the maggots are eating scumbag Sean'. In a bizarre development a hitman was videoed taking a lie detector test which he said proved he wasn't involved in the killing of Little. Caolan Smyth would later be convicted and jailed for 20 years for the attempted murder of Kinahan target James 'Mago' Gately, whom he shot a number of times at a petrol station forecourt. At the same time the Little group was imploding, Mr Flashy's mob, known as the Gucci Gang, had also found themselves under attack. From neighbouring Finglas, the group had earned their nickname by outrageously flaunting their wealth on social media. While they had been handed Finglas on a plate from the Kinahan cartel it wasn't long before Flashy found enemies in his own ranks and from rival gangs who he tried to control with threats and intimidation.

While the complex feuds were playing out in north Dublin and Garda resources continued to be stretched, Mr Big took his opportunities where he saw them. While the once-mighty Kinahan cartel had links with all the big mobs, North and South, Mr Big had forged his own connections deep in Ireland's drug territories of the south-west, north-west and into Belfast. He'd a working relationship with the remnants of the McCarthy–Dundons in Limerick, and in Sligo, where dealer Barry Young was operating as a major supplier to Northern drug mobs. Young was relatively low profile, despite a lengthy career in organised crime that had made him an international player. In his early 20s he'd taken on an older drugs mob in his home town of Sligo and then formed his own sub-group when they were dismantled. In 2006 he'd been caught in a graveyard with a large amount of cannabis but instead of fighting his case, he entered a guilty plea and served just four years. When he got out he concentrated on building business with suppliers in Spain and customers in Ireland, North and South, trading guns, cocaine and heroin. He forged a close working relationship with a gang from north Dublin formerly headed up by the missing Sean Dunne who'd disappeared in Alicante at the height of his power. His grouping had been taken over by associates and the relationship provided Young with a direct supply line from Spain to Sligo. He'd also kept close with John Gilligan and regularly visited him in Spain.

In Drogheda, Mr Big had forged a far more complex working relationship with the gang led by Cornelius Price and Owen Maguire. The duo, whose alliance had created a successful cocaine and weapons business following the murders of local dealers Reay and Coddington by Eric 'Lucky' Wilson, had grown rapidly around the lucrative town and north towards the border. While Mr Big was happy to wheel and deal with the pair, he had also aligned himself with them for another reason, a long-term rivalry with his old foe Richie Carberry, whose business had grown steadily since his move out of Dublin and which had the potential to skyrocket if he continued to support a younger crew who believed they could grab control of the patch.

Carberry had been methodically building his footprint in Drogheda since he'd moved to the seaside town of Bettystown, on the eastern coastline, less than ten years before. He'd recognised the money-making potential in the town and its surrounding areas and had aligned himself as a supplier with a number of ambitious young Price–Maguire protégés who'd fallen out with their bosses. He'd been successfully laundering money outside the capital for years. By 2016 he had a new company, RPC Enterprises, operating out of a plush commercial premises in Laytown in County Meath, where his mother-in-law and her partner had moved, but little business went on there. Tensions between the Price–Maguire faction and Carberry's group were growing and tit-for-tat incidents had begun to build up a head of steam, with damage to cars and graffiti being sprayed.

Carberry was well aware of the fearsome enemies he was about to take on, but he was also prepared to go to war for the big prize of the drug turf at stake. Cornelius Price was a vicious Traveller mob boss who operated from a fortified compound in Gormanston, County Meath containing a number of mobile homes and caravans where his associates lived. It was the last place that 34-year-old Willie Maughan and 21-year-old Ana Varslavane were seen alive before going missing in April 2015. The couple had been living on the compound but were planning to move out, back to where Willie's parents, Helen and Joe, lived in Tallaght in Dublin. They were due to meet Willie's mother when they vanished without trace. Gardaí immediately suspected that they had been killed on the orders of Price, fearful that they knew too much about his activities. Their bodies, officers suspected, had been disposed of after they'd been killed at the compound. Helen and Joe Maughan didn't take their son's disappearance lying down, despite the terrifying reputation of the man who'd ordered his death. They searched fields and ditches around Gormanston in the weeks after the disappearances and begged local farmers and landowners to check outbuildings. They also went on *Crimecall* to appeal for information, making the case a high-profile double murder hunt. Joe said: 'My son knew something that he should not have known and that is why they have been taken away.' The couple revealed that shortly before 3pm on the day Willie and Ana disappeared, 14 April, Ana had made a chilling phone call, crying: 'Help, help, help', with sounds of choking audible in the background. Joe continued to give interviews to keep his son and his girlfriend's case alive, saying:

If I have to get my son back with his eyes closed, I want to lay him to rest with his brother. If she comes back with her eyes closed I'll lay her to rest in a proper manner as well. Willie was offered to do something. He has a conscience. They were asking him to kill somebody. They thought he was a junkie or a heroin addict, that he would jump on the money.

The constant media attention angered Price, who set about teaching Joe and Helen to keep their mouths shut. First he had messages relayed to the grieving parents; grisly stories claiming that the couple had been tortured before their bodies were dissolved in acid. Then he took his intimidation a step further and one day after Joe had appealed again for information about his missing son, the grave of Willie's brother at Bohernabreena Cemetery was dug up in the early hours of the morning. Despite the desecration of the final resting place of Michael 'Bobby' Maughan, who had died of meningitis aged 30, brave Joe kept up his campaign, telling Adrian Kennedy's 98FM *Dublin Talks*:

These people are from Balbriggan and Drogheda that are involved in my son's disappearance and what happened in the early hours of Wednesday morning . . . They're trying to intimidate me because I was in a national newspaper during the week. This was intimidation, this was a threat, they're trying to take my son's body out of a grave. If I get my son back and his girlfriend back, I'll let the law take its course from there. I've been threatened, my family has been threatened in previous months by those people and I still won't back down. I won't leave this earth till I get my son, and if

I have to leave, my family will carry on until we get answers for William and Ana.

Three men had entered the cemetery some time after 2am to carry out the act, although they stopped short of removing Michael's remains from his coffin. Helen said she was heartbroken by the loss of her two sons and described the scene of the unearthed grave as 'like something out of a horror film'. She said:

> It was my worst nightmare, when I looked at that grave and I had to walk away from there when the gravediggers were filling it in – it felt like burying my son all over again. That broke my heart and it'll always break my heart, but Bobby's my son, I love him, and William is still my son, I love him and Ana. I will still fight for justice for William and Ana, but what they did to my son's grave was like something out of a horror film. If I back down from this now, I'm giving into this gang of scum, if I let them get the better of me, they'll do it to another family.

The murder of Willie and Ana was suspected to lie at the heart of another murder that the Price crew was believed to have perpetrated. Along with Owen Maguire, Price had gone to war with drug lord Benny Whitehouse, who was supplying drugs in Louth and north County Dublin when he was shot dead in 2013 after refusing to pay a €30,000 'drug tax' to the Price organisation. Price was furious because Whitehouse had stopped buying drugs from him and switched to a new supplier. He'd been warned a number of times that his life was in danger, and he was killed at nine o'clock on a September morning after dropping his child to school. Price was suspected of bringing a hitman in from the UK to carry out the job as a lesson to anyone else who refused to deal with him. Later, two of Whitehouse's brothers were warned their lives were in danger too.

By 2017 a number of things happened which would lay out a roadmap for the murder and mayhem to come. Following growing tensions within the Maguire gang it officially split, with two brothers on one side, along with their sidekick Paul Crosby; and Owen Maguire and his loyalists on the other. While Cornelius Price gave his support firmly to Maguire he was facing charges of having driven a car at a police officer and in February of that year found himself locked up in Wheatfield Prison. With his violent sidekick incarcerated, Maguire was left exposed and vulnerable as rivalries with his former protégés grew, along with their confidence. Carberry quickly pinned his allegiance to the brothers' faction, helping to supply them with drugs, weapons and advice. For more than a year there was a spate of attacks on members of both sides, with unspeakable life-altering injuries meted out and several homes destroyed, as the community around them looked on in horror.

At the same time Robbie Lawlor started to spend more and more time with his brother-in-law Richie Carberry and in the County Louth and Meath areas where his mother Celia was now living. His own domestic situation had added to the frequency of his visits north of the capital – he'd split up with his partner Rachel Kirwan after a long and volatile relationship. Lawlor was in his 30s but increasingly chaotic and a very heavy user of steroids and cocaine. He'd been in and out of the prison system since his early 20s and regularly fought with fellow lags. On the outside he raged against anyone he perceived had slighted him or owed him money. In January 2016 he'd ended up in the Court of Appeal, trying to get some time off a 32-month sentence he had been handed down after pleading guilty to being in the possession of stolen property. The evidence gave an insight into the precarious way he existed and the kind of crimes he committed to earn his day-to-day cash. It also showed an impulsive personality and the type of risks he was willing to take in order to keep himself in pocket money. During the robbery in question, in March 2013, he hadn't strayed too far from home, threatening staff at a McDonald's restaurant in Donaghmede shopping centre, where he was a regular customer. There was about €10,000 in the cash box, which happened to be fitted with a tracking device, and gardaí found it later that day in a field at Kinsealy. A few days later gardaí spotted Lawlor in Darndale posting a package into a house and when they recovered it, they found it contained €3,420 in banknotes covered in blue dye from the McDonald's cash box. Lawlor had pleaded guilty to possessing stolen property and during the appeal the court was told how, at 31 years old, he had an incredible 125 previous convictions.

Lawlor was released from jail just as Price started to serve his time and he immediately focused his attention on Mr Big, who had become a powerhouse in his old neighbourhood of Coolock and who had vocalised his hatred for Carberry. In different circumstances Lawlor would have been of use to Mr Big, such was his relish for killing, but blood bonds with Carberry meant that his loyalties lay with his brother-in-law. Carberry, like Mr Big, was an opportunist and knew that his rival was supportive of the Price–Maguire faction, who were by now his mortal enemies in a war for control. He knew that the fight for Drogheda would be pursued to the death and he considered the threat that Mr Big could pose to him in the coming years. Like a chess player, he planned his next move with precision and cunning. In February 2018 Kenneth Finn, Mr Big's best friend and trusted hitman, was sitting in a car outside a house at Moatview Gardens when he was shot. He died a few days later at Beaumont Hospital. Donna Clarke, Finn's partner, later told an inquest that at around 6.30pm on 25 February Finn had told her he was going out and would be back in 20 minutes, but he didn't say where he was off to. At 8pm, she revealed, she had had a call from a friend to say he'd been shot. A resident of Moatview, Jean McKeever was forced to describe how she had found Finn lying in her front garden after she heard another family member screaming. She'd heard a loud bang shortly before that, which she described as being like a firework, but as she called the ambulance service and tried to stop the flow of blood from Finn's head it was clear that he wouldn't survive the shooting. The coroner, Dr Myra Cullinane, said a post-mortem on Finn's body had concluded that he had died as a result of a wound from a single bullet, which was lodged in his brain.

Like most professionals, Finn had mixed with his own and had been a close pal of the recently murdered Hutch gangster Jason 'Buda' Molyneaux and the murdered gangland gunman Jamie Tighe Ennis, who had been shot dead in Moatview a year earlier.

Both had been linked to the horrific double murders of the innocent Antoinette Corbally and Clinton Shannon in Ballymun in Dublin some months before. The intended target of that attack was the notorious criminal Derek 'Bottler' Devoy, Antoinette's brother, who'd escaped over a wall having dropped the baby he was holding when the gunmen produced their weapons.

Antoinette was a mother of six and had been hit in the head and torso in the hallway of the family home on Balbutcher Drive during the crazed attack. Her pregnant daughter Andrea, who was 18 at the time, was injured when a bullet grazed her and had witnessed the attack, while locksmith Shannon was sitting outside in a car. Antoinette was the second of the Devoy siblings to be murdered. In 2014 her brother Mickey Devoy was killed by a member of the Kinahan drug cartel. 'Bottler' Devoy, then 37, was uninjured in the gun attack that took his sister's life but was hell-bent on revenge. He was a dangerous criminal who had spent eight years locked up for the attempted armed robbery of a post office in 2006 and for the non-fatal drive-by shooting of two of his neighbours in Ballymun in 2005. When Devoy had been released from jail in February 2015, gardaí had to draw up a special security plan just to keep him alive, which involved multiple armed checkpoints close to his Ballymun home. Months later he'd fled the country and was in the process of moving more than €100,000 to a bank in Britain when the account was frozen by detectives in Dublin. Devoy had returned to Ireland to take on CAB, which was hoping to secure the money as proceeds of crime, and to settle old scores regarding the murder of his older brother Mickey. When his sister was shot too he was approached by the Kinahan organisation and told he would have their logistics and firearms backing should he wish to get back at the two suspected gunmen, Molyneaux and Tighe Ennis, who were aligned to the Hutch organisation. The Kinahans were being opportunistic rather than generous. Down massive manpower due to multiple senior members and hit teams being behind bars, they were happy to help with the murder of Molyneaux and Tighe Ennis because of their links to the Hutch side.

The reasons for the murder of Kenneth Finn were not initially clear. His links to Molyneaux and Tighe Ennis was one of the first possible motives examined, but experienced detectives knew it didn't make sense that he would be a target because of a simple case of friendship. And besides, there was no known animosity between the Mr Big organisation and the Kinahan cartel, who'd facilitated the other two murders. Another theory was that Mr Big had ordered the hit on his own friend, but while he'd been known to conduct in-house clearing before, intelligence suggested that he was absolutely livid at the murder of his pal and best marksman. Mr Big didn't go to Finn's funeral, but his presence was keenly felt throughout the ceremony, as Finn was remembered as a loyal friend whose death would not be forgotten.

Officers soon started to focus on Robbie Lawlor and the links to increasing tensions in Drogheda. They also suspected that he had easy access to a new stash of heavy-duty firearms. Months after the Finn murder, an underling of Lawlor was found with a cache of guns, including a submachine firearm and four handguns, when he fled from a Garda checkpoint and dumped a bag as he ran. Reports suggested that Lawlor had survived a number of assassination attempts himself as he lurched between Coolock and the Louth and Meath area, where he stayed between properties, and it soon appeared the murder of Finn could have been a 'kill or be killed' strategy on behalf of Lawlor and under the direction of his brother-in-law, Richie Carberry.

At that point, gardaí in Drogheda were heavily focused on the feud and the relationships between the various protagonists. They had carried out a lengthy assessment of the situation and knew they were facing a brutal gang war as terrifying attacks increased between the two sides of the divide, now known as the Price–Maguire faction and the anti-Price–Maguire grouping. They knew they had to disarm and immobilise both sides in as many ways as they could, and hitting them in the pocket was one key area they were focused on. In April 2018, a series of raids were conducted by local police, CAB and other high-powered units. They focused on the Price–Maguire faction and moved in on 22 properties, seizing €30,000 in cash, mobile phones, vehicles and a 'tick list' of drug debts.

With Lawlor the chief suspect in the Finn murder and his constant presence around Drogheda he found himself under closer Garda scrutiny and undoubtedly his behaviour was increasingly neurotic and fuelled by a diet of cocaine and steroids. He was fast becoming a liability to anyone who crossed his path. His former girlfriend Rachel Kirwan was by then living in terror of her ex-partner and the father of her two kids. The couple had been together more than ten years and during their relationship she had shown a fierce loyalty to him. But she was scared of him too and she'd once made a complaint that he'd beaten her, but never followed up on the accusations. After their breakup and in the run-up to Christmas 2017, Lawlor had discovered that Kirwan was seeing someone else, a Coolock man called Derek Mitchell, and he wasn't happy about it. He was even more furious when he found out that his children had become close to Derek and his mum Fiona, who regularly had them around at her house.

Just before 1am on 26 May 2018, Fiona Mitchell heard her beloved dog Chopper 'going mad barking' in the back garden of her home in Priorswood. She went to investigate and when she looked out of her kitchen window, she saw two men on the back wall. When she went to the patio doors to get a closer look and stared out, she was suddenly confronted by the sight of a man whose face she instantly recognised staring back at her. He was holding a gun. Like something straight out of a Hollywood horror film, Fiona bolted for the hallway, slamming and locking the kitchen door behind her. As she ran, she screamed at her other son Jason, who was playing computer games in the sitting room, to get out of the house. Jason didn't need to be told twice and jumped through a window into the front garden. In the meantime, his mother was running through the front door, the sound of gunshots exploding behind her. In the aftermath the gardaí found four bullets; one was lodged in the decking in the back garden, one was located in the kitchen and another was found in the front garden. A ballistics inspection was able to tell that it had been fired from the kitchen and had gone through the front door. The fourth bullet had killed Fiona's German shepherd, Chopper, whose barking had ultimately saved her life. Fiona would later tell a courtroom how she knew for sure that the man who climbed over her back wall that night and stormed into her house firing a gun was Robbie Lawlor. Fiona had heard bits about the reputation of Lawlor and had been wary when her son Derek had told her he was dating his ex, but nonetheless she had forged a close relationship with Rachel and had become a sympathetic ear for her as she told stories of intimidation, threats and beatings at Lawlor's hands during their long relationship. Rachel had confided in Fiona that Lawlor was driven crazy by her new relationship with Derek and had tried to force her to dump him. In her statements in the immediate aftermath of the incident, she told gardaí that Lawlor had planned to kill Fiona first and leave Derek grieving for a fortnight before putting him out of his misery. She also said that Lawlor had threatened to 'blow [Derek's] head off, blow his ma's head off and leave him with nothing'. She said the threats were 'constant from the minute he found out' about herself and Derek.

On the night of the attack on Fiona Mitchell's house, Kirwan had received a phone call from Detective Garda Noel Smith. He told her that she should be careful, that Lawlor was 'extremely agitated'. He'd met the volatile criminal at about 10.25pm in Laytown, County Meath, near the house where he was then living with his mother. Lawlor was dressed in black leggings, black runners and a black jacket and Detective Smith noticed that he was agitated and aggressive and behaving erratically. The detective was so concerned that he went to Lawlor's home and spoke to his mother, Celia Dillon, who said she too was worried about her son. As a result, he'd made the decision to alert both the Armed Support Unit and Rachel Kirwan. In her first statement Kirwan told gardaí that the phone call had left her nervous and she had a 'feeling he was going to hurt me and Derek'. She'd spent most of the rest of the night on the phone to Fiona, ringing every 15 to 20 minutes to make sure she was okay. It was during one of those phone calls, Kirwan said, that she heard a dog barking in the background at Fiona's house and she told gardaí that she heard Fiona say, 'Hang on, why is that dog barking?' and then she heard her screaming: 'He's here, he's here, it's happening!' The next thing she heard, she told the officers, was gunshots. 'I thought she was dead,' she said. 'I thought she was gone. If she had died, I would have had to carry that around for the rest of my life.'

As gardaí began to put together their case against Lawlor in the hopes of placing him into custody he carried on regardless, moving between north Dublin and into his Louth and Meath territories. Officers were sure he was capable of killing again and worked against the clock to prepare a file for the Director of Public Prosecutions about the attack at Fiona Mitchell's home. They knew the clock was ticking on the time bomb that was Robbie Lawlor and that his next move could escalate things in Drogheda to a critical level.

CHAPTER FOUR

A Murder and a Town at War

On 5 July 2018, Owen Maguire was at home at his family's halting site on Cement Road. It was after midnight and he was planning to go out to meet a pal who'd been released from prison when a car drove in. As he approached the vehicle a masked gunman opened the passenger door and without warning shot him, hitting him three times in the body. As he fell, the gunman stood over him, lifted his face covering and attempted to unleash what would be the fatal bullets into the injured mob boss. But the gun jammed. Before the gunman fled the scene, the injured Maguire recognised his would-be killer as Robbie Lawlor. Despite being in agony, Maguire managed to call for help and was rushed to Our Lady of Lourdes Hospital where he underwent immediate surgery. The news for his family was mixed; while Owen would survive, he had been left with catastrophic injuries and a bullet was lodged in his spine. As medics worked on Maguire, checkpoints were set up on the roads leaving Drogheda and a Volkswagen Passat was seen passing one on the M1 with a flat tyre and travelling at speed. Officers gave chase, pulled the car over as it headed towards the border and the driver got out wearing just underwear and emitting a strong smell of petrol. He gave a false name and address and spun a story of having to siphon petrol from another car as he'd been running low. Robbie Lawlor was arrested but he had disposed of the firearm.

The shooting had been a planned attack and Lawlor had displayed his usual calmness as he shot Maguire in the legs, making him fall to the ground, and in the wrist so he couldn't grab for any firearm he might have been carrying. But when he had moved in to finish him off with his signature bullet to the head the gun had failed and Lawlor had been forced to flee, leaving Maguire writhing in agony on the ground. With Cornelius Price still in prison, Maguire had been more vulnerable to Carberry, who had decided it was time to send Lawlor in for the kill, but now that he had survived it was nowhere near checkmate. As Maguire's condition was stabilised, armed gardaí surrounded the hospital where he was being treated for fear that Lawlor, whom officers had been forced to release from custody after his roadside arrest, would come back and try to finish the job. Despite his near miss with the law and the fact that he had been apprehended so close to the kill, Lawlor had left custody with an air of confidence and menace that indicated he was capable of anything. His proximity to the scene of the shooting and the fact that he smelled of petrol would not be enough to convince a court that he had been the gunman who tried to kill Maguire and the Gardaí knew that the victim would not be co-operating with any inquiry. There was no question but Maguire and his pal Price were already plotting a bloody revenge for the brazen assassination attempt. The need to get Lawlor off the street and into custody was never more pressing and officers working the Fiona Mitchell case doubled down on their efforts to get charges in relation to that attempted murder. Finally the Director of Public Prosecutions gave the green light to bring Lawlor before the courts on a driving offence, enough to hold him while the situation calmed. But Lawlor's incarceration gave just the briefest respite to gardaí in Drogheda as they faced the fall-out from the attempt on Owen Maguire's life.

Ironically it was behind bars that the feud would take its next sinister twist and one which would have ripple effects on a whole host of lives. Finally charged with the events at Fiona Mitchell's home, Lawlor agitated for release on bail but this was refused and in October of 2018 he found himself in the same prison as Cornelius Price. As inmates cleared up after a meal one day the mob boss approached the hitman and extended his hand to Lawlor, holding on to it while two other inmates attacked him with prison shivs (makeshift knives). Lawlor was humiliated and badly injured and had to be have 29 stitches. If the pair hadn't been mortal enemies before, they were now, and the stage was set for a theatre of terror between two of Ireland's most dangerous criminals.

Just months before the 'Judas handshake', Chief Superintendent Christy Mangan had arrived in Drogheda for what would be the final phase of his lengthy career. A native of County Meath, he thought he had intimate knowledge of the town near where he had grown up and where he had reared his own family. Mangan was looking forward to what would be the final challenge of his four decades in An Garda Síochána and which would lead him to his retirement. But instead of a quiet landing, the veteran drug squad detective and murder case investigator quickly realised that policing and protecting Drogheda was going to be a challenge like none before it. Mangan was known as a good cop, hands-on despite the rank he had achieved, and always conscious of the reality of the beat, despite having his own comfortable office. From his headquarters in the town he quickly established that the prosperous commuter town that had welcomed foreign investors and a young new workforce was on 'the brink of destruction' and was the epicentre of a brutal gang war the likes of which had rarely been seen outside Dublin or Limerick.

As Mangan assessed the situation he knew he had one stark problem – the town's location. In Dublin, officers could rely on quick backup and quick access to specialist and armed units should any incident occur, but the County Louth division was not so well resourced. On the ground, Mangan could see that there was a split between the once all-powerful Price and Maguire crime group and that a breakaway younger faction populated by impulsive and violent thugs was threatening the old order. At the heart of the dispute was both a fight for supremacy and also the lucrative cocaine turf stretching from the town and along the eastern seaboard to the border. It was turf that had exploded in value hand-in-hand with the prosperity of Drogheda and its environs. The gangs weren't pushing cocaine onto a reluctant customer base; instead, a young, educated and skilled workforce with disposable income was feeding a multi-million-euro trade that was making the mob leaders incredibly rich and powerful and giving them the impression that they were in charge. It wasn't just the ambitious youngsters who'd worked for the Price and Maguire outfits who were eyeing up the territory. The proximity of the area to north Dublin and its fast-growing population had meant that many significant players from the drugs trade had moved and settled in the small townlands and villages that surrounded the town. Mangan knew that Carberry, who had the volatile Robbie Lawlor in his armoury, was the most significant blow-in and that he gave a powerful backing to the younger grouping. Looking back over the crime reports Mangan could see that incidents of attacks on houses and petrol bombings were spiralling, while those who owed drug debts were reporting high levels of intimidation and threat. He knew that all the ingredients for a conflagration were in place and it wouldn't be long before the gangs would start shooting one another.

One of Mangan's first observations was that the gangs appeared to be operating with impunity without the kind of police operations that had been used against the Dublin and Limerick mobs; the relentless targeting of gang members and their weapons stashes, and the intelligence-led seizures of their drugs. In Drogheda the gangs had enjoyed years of doing as they pleased and growing their power and war chests. If they were caught it was usually luck on the Garda's part and nothing more organised. Mangan recognised that the future development of the town was under pressure, with the groups brazenly targeting a building company and threatening to kidnap the owners. Investment in Drogheda was vital to the continued success and growth of the town as one of the main commuter cities outside Dublin, but criminality was sure to scare away those eyeing it up as a centre of employment and opportunity. Drogheda was an excellent location for drug dealers because of its position between north Dublin and the border, and as the new chief examined the situation he knew his segue to retirement was going to be anything but quiet. 'When I went there in 2017 I got a very quick sense of what the realities were there as regards to crime,' he says.

> It would have appeared that cocaine use was absolutely rampant and you could quickly identify who the main drug dealers were. At that time there was one very dominant grouping known locally as the Price–Maguire OCG and they were in control of the supply of all illicit drugs right from the border to Dundalk and up to Balbriggan, which is a fair chunk of an area to be controlling because it has a huge monetary value to the people involved. It is a multi-million-euro business. So I carried out an assessment of what the crime situation was and at that time it became obvious that there was a falling out between the main group and some of the younger members of it had evolved into the anti-Maguire Group, and that is what I would call them for easy reference from then on. They started basically having fist fights, on the streets, cat calling, they were going on social media and taunting each other and then it evolved that some of the younger members of the anti-Price–Maguire group got a couple of bad hidings and they didn't take it too well because they were losing a lot of the fights on the streets. They started to target members of the Price–Maguire group. They started by damaging cars; they

were smashing windscreens, throwing petrol bombs at cars and then that evolved into attacking houses and at one stage in the feud we had over 34 houses which were badly destroyed as a result of the activities of both sides. Then they started to threaten each other's girlfriends and partners and were threatening to throw acid in their faces. There had been a lot of serious crime committed by the original grouping, which was the Price–Maguire wing; they had been involved in murders, one of the earliest was that of Benjamin Whitehouse, he had been murdered in Balbriggan and then also Willie Maughan and Ana Varslavane, both went missing and are now recorded as a double murder. That is what we were dealing with at the time and we certainly realised that we had a huge problem on our hands because normally, you know, criminal groupings, when they fall out, they come to a realisation that if they don't stop they will end up in prison or they would end up losing a lot of the profits, but in this case there was no relenting. They simply had made a decision that it was going to be a basic fight to the death. So we then had to devise a plan on how to deal with it while dealing with your normal policing issues.

Mangan saw his primary function as keeping the people of Louth safe. A huge air of paranoia was developing, and not only in the criminal underworld. Locals were finding themselves being intimidated for drug debts, often built up by their children, and more and more stories emerged of terrified families handing over huge sums of money in order to stop the threats. To add to the problem, a lot of the main players involved on opposing sides of the gangs were intermarried, related and with intimate knowledge of each other's living arrangements and habitual movements. They were also living in small estates where their families and girlfriends were obvious targets. Mangan devised an emergency plan as he began to lobby for more money and more boots on the ground. He cancelled annual leave for all gardaí in Drogheda and the greater Louth area, sending out a directive to all officers that he wouldn't allow holidays to be taken while the threat loomed. He worried that such an extreme measure would not go down well with members of the force, but the majority of officers working the beat were also living with their families in the area, were invested in their community and were well aware that the situation was becoming critical. Nobody complained. Mangan was surprised but buoyed by the fact that it wasn't just him who saw the starkness of the situation. To maintain law and order, gardaí knew they were on a war footing and that every shoulder was needed at the wheel to take on the gangs. The decorated officer had worked in other areas where he was faced with high levels of crime and feuding, but that was in a city environment where loads of resources were to hand. 'If you get in a bit of bother in some part of Dublin you will have a car there in a matter of minutes but if you get into difficulty in parts of Louth it might take twenty minutes to get a car to you, so it's a different environment to be working in,' he would later explain.

With his top officers, Mangan devised Operation Stratus, which would interact with all the State agencies in Louth: the Health Service Executive; Tusla, the child welfare service; and the court services. The county council was brought to the table as it was their social houses that were being burnt out and their properties that were being sprayed with highly incendiary graffiti, with rival gang members calling each other out as 'rats' or 'touts' and making derogatory comments about their partners. Basic issues like removing the artwork and installing new lighting in some of the housing estates were discussed and improvements were made. Operation Stratus focused on trying to put a bit of pride back into the communities so that locals actively wanted to live in their areas, confident that the drug gangs were the enemies and not the State. Meetings were held and at one a mother came to Mangan and told him that she was absolutely terrified to let her children out to play on the streets, she was so afraid of what could happen to them. She described an incident when children were out playing one evening and found firearms and pipe bombs. Mangan would later say:

> So matters like that were happening and we were in constant contact with our local politicians who, to be fair, were of huge support and benefit to me as the manager of the police up there and the resources. They did play a huge part recovering from the position we were in, because we were absolutely on our knees, we were. One night we had seven major crimes which took place and normally you have to appoint a garda to mind the scene, that is the basics of crime investigation, and Superintendent Andy Watters rang me at 5am to tell me that he had run out of gardaí. There were no more left. So when that happens, certainly, you get an understanding of what we were facing.

When the shootings started the situation intensified. Two major murder enquiries were already under way in the division, those of Garda Tony Golden and his colleague Detective Garda Adrian Donohoe. Both had been killed in the line of duty. In 2013 Detective Garda Adrian Donohoe was shot dead as armed robbers held up the credit union in the village of Lordship on the Cooley Peninsula. Golden had been shot dead in 2015 while responding to a domestic abuse case in a house at Omeath. Garda Golden, an affable and popular officer, left behind a wife and three young children. On the night he died, he'd been on duty when Siobhan Phillips came to make a complaint of domestic abuse. He'd travelled with her to the house she shared with Crevan Mackin, a dissident republican, and had gone in to help her gather her things. Her father was waiting outside when he heard gunshots and immediately called 999. But Garda Golden was discovered dead at the scene. Gunman Adrian Crevan Mackin had killed the officer and critically injured his own ex-partner Siobhan Phillips before turning the gun on himself. Mangan explained:

> If you have a crime like murder you could have fifty or sixty staff taken up taking statements and interviewing people, so a lot of resources goes into a major investigation and we were also in the midst of ATM robberies, we had a huge amount of that on the border and we were heavily involved in the capital murder investigation of Detective Garda Adrian Donohoe and also we were dealing with the murder of Garda Tony Golden. So each of those major cases has huge resource implications for you as a manager. When you have only limited resources, and they are involved in those other cases, it leaves very little left to be out on the streets so you don't have the boots on the ground which is where they are needed. You

need a very visible presence in certain housing estates to make sure anti-social behaviour is not taking place and that people aren't out riding scramblers across the green areas and damaging things belonging to the community. We had an incident where a local soccer club was attacked and all their equipment was damaged.

Following the murder attempt on Maguire, tensions were at boiling point. Over the following months, intelligence suggested, each side was gathering reinforcements, with criminals based in the UK coming home to help in the fight. Maguire put up €60,000 for the murder of the brothers who had once served in his ranks and others in their inner circle. With Robbie Lawlor in jail, the plan for his demise would have to be put on the long finger. Gardaí responded by raiding the halting site and recovering €270,000 in cash. Soon afterwards petrol bombs were thrown at the home of a rival of Maguire and twelve shots were fired into a house at Moneymore estate where Maguire's former protégés lived. When a viable explosive device was placed in the car belonging to a girlfriend of a key member of the anti-Price–Maguire group, tensions rose even further and 24 hours later one of Maguire's young crew was kidnapped, taken to a house in the Moneymore estate, stripped, beaten and sliced in a bathroom. Gardaí were called to the scene and rescued the youngster. They arrested 26-year-old Dean Thornton at the scene, who was subsequently convicted for his role in the brutal attack. Later, premises used by the anti-Maguire faction were set alight and a caravan at Cement Road was set on fire in retaliation. Petrol bombings, shooting incidents and intimidation followed as Gardaí estimated more than 150 individuals were involved on both sides.

In the middle of the tensions a WhatsApp video showing Paul Crosby taunting the injured Owen Maguire began to circulate. Just as it had with the young gangs of Coolock, social media was playing a role and heightening the tensions. Crosby started the call by introducing himself to Maguire and asking the mob boss if he remembered him. 'Never met you in me life,' came the response. 'Just ringing to see how you are getting on, are ye all right?' Crosby asked Maguire, who responded that he was good. 'I was just thinking about it for the last while man, it is hard on top isn't it? C'mere, listen . . . How ye getting on, all right? Ye still up at the hospital, are ye? The next day or two me and me mates are gonna drop you up a few flowers . . . Ye stuck for anything up there? Do ye need anything?' Maguire responded that he didn't. 'Well . . . are you stuck for any auld nappies or that now? If you want I'll bring you up a few . . . There is animosity between us two, yeah? Honest to God we should go for an auld walk, Owen, one of the days and sort things out . . . I wouldn't be pushing your chair, get one of them electric ones would you not?' Crosby went on to make derogatory sexual comments about Maguire's partner Francine and his sisters. 'How's your brother Brendan? How's he getting on? Tell him I'm asking for him . . . Must be hard going from the top to eight stone wringing wet, man . . . Did you get them auld hubcaps as well? . . . Are you pimping out your ride, man? . . . You can run your mouth there but all said and done you'll never walk again, will ye? . . . It must be hard to come to terms with that. But if you could rewind time would you not have been a bullying bastard.' Maguire warned: 'We had you down as a half clever lad but look what you are after doing . . . You'll never live in this town again.'

The chilling exchange was shared thousands of times through WhatsApp groups and placed on social media, inflaming the situation. It ended with Maguire warning that his 'buddy' would be out in a few weeks. In fact Cornelius Price was due to be released from prison in May 2019, but officers were already formulating a policing plan to handle the carnage that was expected once he walked free. Price had been disciplined for using a phone to issue threats from behind bars and to organise drug deals but he was also mobilising support from his associates in the UK to give him back-up as soon as he got out of prison. Meanwhile Richie Carberry was increasing his support for the anti Price-Maguire faction, encouraging them to hit out again at their rivals before Price got out.

While Owen Maguire continued to receive medical attention and protection in hospital as he recovered from his injuries and from surgery, his younger brother Brendan became a clear target. In February 2019, as he sat in a car at the M1 retail park just outside Drogheda he was shot three times and was rushed to the same hospital as Owen to receive complex surgery on his neck and face. The VW Passat used in the shooting was discovered to have been stolen from a north County Dublin suburb and had been hidden while the Maguires' rivals planned the attack. It was found burnt out at the seaside town of Seapoint that evening. A month later Richie Carberry's house in Bettystown came under attack for the first time. The 39-year-old had just arrived home when a lone gunman approached the house and shot at the doors and the front window before escaping in a car found burnt out just outside the posh Castlemartin estate where he lived. Days later there was a firebomb attack in the Moneymore estate in Drogheda, extensively damaging the ground floor of a home.

All the gang activity in Drogheda was undoubtedly costing money, and both sides had turned on their communities to raise funds. At a Drogheda Joint Policing Committee meeting, local councillor Ruairí Ó Murchú said he was aware of a man who paid one of the gangs €40,000 to clear a debt they said was owed by his daughter. 'People are afraid, they are embarrassed, they just want it to go away, so they pay,' he said. Mangan responded by appointing a special inspector to deal solely with families in debt. He warned families not to pay the gangs when money was demanded: 'We want to engage with families. Drug dealers won't go away. Once they know the tap is open, they will keep coming back.' With the impending release of Price, and acting on intelligence that Owen Maguire had hidden weapons there, gardaí moved in to search fields near his fortified home. Sniffer dogs searched the fields but despite trawling through ditches the gardaí came away empty-handed.

In April, at Hardmans Gardens, another innocent local escaped death when one of nine shots fired from a busy street came within inches of hitting her. The target was a senior criminal with links to Maguire who was near the scene, but a 36-year-old man ended up in hospital. A video showed how lucky the female passerby was to escape with her life. It followed another spate of assaults and petrol bomb attacks. Local Fine Gael councillor

Richard Culhane likened the situation to that which had gripped Limerick during the height of the wars between the McCarthy–Dundons and their rivals in the Keane–Collopy faction. 'This feud will go on, by the very nature of these feuds, until they're put behind bars as what happened in Limerick. It is only a matter of time before an innocent victim gets caught up in this,' he said.

The situation in Limerick had finally abated but not without a huge effort by the State. Among many things learned was that dismantling warring gangs was not something that happened overnight and it could not be achieved without massive resources.

The Dundon brothers, like the Price–Maguire faction, came from the Travelling community and were fiercely loyal to each other. The first to be jailed for life was Dessie, who was one of five members of the McCarthy–Dundon gang convicted in 2003 of the murder of Kieran Keane and the attempted murder and false imprisonment of Owen Treacy. At that point more than forty members on both sides of the divide had been jailed in relation to feud activity, but worse was to come. Wayne, John and Ger Dundon were free men and continued to wreak chaos on Limerick through intimidation and murder for almost a decade more. They forced families out of the Ballinacurra Weston area where they lived and took over their homes, they attempted to import rocket launchers from Europe and showed contempt for the Gardaí and the judiciary. John Dundon had openly threatened witness Owen Treacy during his uncle's murder trial during which he gave evidence about how he had been left for dead on a roadside by the mob. Jailed for four years, John beat another murder rap for the assassination of nightclub bouncer Brian

Fitzgerald before he was eventually convicted of the 2008 killing of innocent rugby player Shane Geoghegan, who had been shot five times by hapless hitman Barry Doyle. When Wayne had a heated dispute with a barman, Ryan Lee, he threatened to kill him and was jailed for ten years. But later he targeted his cousin, businessman Roy Collins, shot dead at Coin Castle Amusement in 2009. Wayne pleaded not guilty to killing Collins but in 2014 the Special Criminal Court found that he had ordered the murder from prison and sentenced him to life. A €300 million government plan – the Limerick Regeneration Framework Implementation Plan – followed. It was aimed at tackling poverty, social exclusion and crime and focused on the rebuilding of Moyross, Weston, Southhill and St Mary's Park estates. With his three brothers serving mandatory sentences for murder, the future of the Dundon mob lay with Ger, who'd moved in and out of the UK and Ireland while the Keane grouping strengthened their hold over the city and began to build up a slick money-laundering operation linked to the car industry.

As the war raged in Drogheda, Mangan had to make some tough decisions and at one point was close to declaring the situation an emergency.

> The incidents were so bad that I [gave] serious consideration to calling in the army because we didn't have the armed resources to deal with this. People were getting shot. I gave very serious consideration to seeking the support of the army, that isn't something you do lightly. We are supposed to be a civilised society and the army would only come in as an aid to the civil power in very serious situations, such as war, and

that is something that I definitely considered. I didn't have the staff to deal with what we were dealing with or any of the major situations.

One week before the release of Cornelius Price from prison, on 18 May 2019 the Gardaí scored a huge coup when they arrested the volatile Paul Crosby after a high-speed chase. He was taken into custody, where he was charged with arson, which took him off the streets while the fight continued. Throughout that summer there were attempted drive-by shootings, fist fights and intimidation of locals for money, but the next key event would leave Richie Carberry wondering if he had bitten off more than he could chew. On 27 August his associate Keith Brannigan was fitting decking at his mobile home on the Ashling Caravan Park at scenic Clogherhead in County Louth when he was shot a number of times in broad daylight. It was the end of summer and families were enjoying their last few days of freedom before they returned from their holiday homes for the school year. Some of the spray of bullets had struck cars outside a nearby grocery store and post office. For the first time a senior member of the Catholic Church weighed in to appeal to the gangs to 'desist' from violence. The Auxiliary Bishop of the Archdiocese of Armagh, Bishop Michael Router, condemned the murder of Brannigan, saying:

> Such violence and disregard for life is always appalling but for such an act to take place in a holiday camp where people were enjoying the last days of summer and near to where children was playing is truly shocking. News reports linked this murder to the ongoing feud between rival gangs in Drogheda and

therefore the threat of reprisals is, unfortunately, a real one. Such a cycle of violence will only lead to further tragedy and loss of life so I would appeal for those involved to desist and consider the futility of their actions.

In Bettystown, Richie Carberry began to weigh up his position. With Cornelius Price out of prison, the Maguire grouping had the backing and strength they needed to make another move on him. He was lucky he had survived months earlier when a gunman came to the door of his home, and with his brother-in-law Robbie Lawlor facing serious charges in relation to the attempted murder of Fiona Mitchell, Carberry didn't have the firepower he needed to defend himself.

Carberry had taken his family to Bettystown for a new life. He'd gambled that the young guns of the anti-Maguire faction had enough to take on and take down the old order, but now they were looking weakened, with Crosby in custody and police relentlessly pursuing the brothers. He'd hoped to take over the turf swiftly, but now it looked like he was in a weak position, so he started to look for a new base for his family in the Manchester area, away from the trouble. Carberry had just signed for a new apartment in the UK city when he was targeted again, and this time he wasn't so lucky. He was closing the gates at his now fortified house in Castlemartin Drive, which he had fitted with bullet-resistant glass and doors, at 11.40pm on 5 November, when he spotted a gunman and turned to run towards his house. His killer opened fire, spraying bullets from a machine pistol. Carberry was hit a number of times in the back and fell to the ground in the driveway of the house. His wife Eileen, Lawlor's older sister, ran to his aid and tried to keep him alive until the paramedics came. He was taken to Our Lady of Lourdes Hospital but died within an hour. While the focus of the murder inquiry was firmly on the Drogheda feud and the activities of Price and Maguire, an agitated Robbie Lawlor reached for the phone in prison. His brother-in-law was only hours dead but already he knew exactly who he was blaming and in a recorded conversation he vowed revenge on Mr Big, the opportunist with a habit of throwing a curve ball when it came to murder. With his trial fixed for the next month he was more determined than ever that no jury would convict him of the attempt to kill Fiona Mitchell. He'd win his freedom and, no matter what, he would exact an unthinkable revenge.

CHAPTER FIVE

The Jury has Decided

Fiona Mitchell was beginning to feel fear. She felt as if her heart was sinking deep into her stomach, her shoulders and neck were completely tensed and her body started to tremble. It was a different feeling from the one she had experienced the night Robbie Lawlor came to kill her – that time pure adrenaline had kicked in and somehow her legs had managed to carry her to safety through the house and out to the front garden. She wasn't so sure they'd work so well now; she felt completely powerless and she had no idea what she was going to do. In front of her Robbie Lawlor was smiling and nodding as the jury foreperson started to read out the first of their five verdicts. The trial had taken just a few weeks, but for Fiona it was a life-or-death case. Now, after she'd stood and testified against him, Lawlor was sitting in the dock looking like the cat that got the cream. The man accused of attempting to murder her and threatening to kill both her and her son Derek a year before was about to walk free, a nightmare scenario that she had pushed to the very back of her mind ever since it was decided that he would face trial. It should have been a cut-and-dried case, but Lawlor's ex-girlfriend Rachel Kirwan had fallen apart in the witness box and had told a very different story from the one in her statements to gardaí. Fiona had hoped the rest of the evidence, including her own testimony about the night Lawlor came for her, would convince the jury to find him guilty as charged and that the trial judge would lock him up for a long time. Nothing about the case had been smooth sailing and there was a lot riding on making the charges stick and keeping Lawlor off the streets. It wasn't just Fiona who was hoping the notorious hitman would be heading to prison; senior officers policing the dangerous Drogheda feud were banking on it too.

As he waited intently for the verdict to be read, Lawlor looked more confident and more demented than ever as he grinned over at the jury, and Fiona had a sinking feeling he could read the room.

The first setback for the investigation had come shortly after the Gardaí had submitted their file to the Director of Public Prosecutions. Since the Gilligan gang had been brought back to Ireland following the murder of Veronica Guerin, the Special Criminal Court – 'the Special', as it was affectionately known by gardaí and court reporters – had become the automatic court for trying all gangland crime and criminals. In fact, following the start of the Kinahan–Hutch feud in 2016, the court had been so busy that a second one had to come on stream and the two would often run different trials at the same time. In 2015 a total of 45 offences had come before the court but that had jumped to 70 in 2019 and would reach 136 in 2020. The use of offences relating to involvement in an OCG laid out in the Criminal Justice (Amendment) Act 2009 was partly responsible for the growing number of cases, despite the reduction in terrorism offences, with membership of an illegal organisation coming before the court just once in 2018.

The 2009 Act had been introduced against a background of gangland violence and was aimed at preventing intimidation of juries and witnesses. New offences included participation in, or contributing to, an OCG – which was automatically referred to the Special. Made up of three judges taken from the District Court, Circuit Court and High Court who came to decisions by majority, the Special had a reputation among the criminal fraternity for frequently handing down guilty verdicts. The previous year, 2018, the Special had reported a conviction rate of 94 per cent, compared to 38 per cent in the circuit courts and 62 per cent in the Central Criminal Court. The Irish Council for Civil Liberties, Amnesty International and the United Nations Commission on Human Rights had sporadically criticised the existence of the court, while Sinn Féin regularly sought its abolition. But the calls had come to nothing and the government's stance on the Special had hardened since the crackdown on organised crime sparked by the Regency Hotel attack and the subsequent Kinahan–Hutch feud. Few beat the system unless there was some extraordinary circumstance. For example, the trial of Patrick Hutch for the murder of David Byrne had spectacularly collapsed earlier that year when the senior investigating officer died suddenly and the State entered a *nolle prosequi* (a dismissal of proceedings). It had, however, taken a while for the new legislation to be used and for gardaí to get used to it. In the ten years since the 2009 amendment, a number of high-profile criminals had got lucky and found themselves before the Circuit Courts, where a jury decided on guilt or innocence. Among them was Mr Big, who'd been charged in relation to a high-profile robbery. The first trial collapsed amid suspicions of jury intimidation, and the second trial was parked when the Director of Public Prosecutions dropped the charges. Mr Big had also got lucky in the North, where he had faced trial for money-laundering and had spent a period of time in custody before the charges were dropped.

While officers investigating Robbie Lawlor's actions at Fiona Mitchell's house had hoped he would be tried by the Special Criminal Court, the offence was not classified as related to organised crime. Although Lawlor was suspected of being a serial hitman with links to Richie Carberry's drug dealing outfit, the events at Mitchell's property had nothing to do with his gang activities and was instead deemed a domestic crime, which meant the trial didn't qualify for the Special. The Director of Public Prosecution's decision to hold the trial in the jury courts meant that Lawlor had a greater chance, statistically, of getting off. It was a blow, but not the end of the world and the Gardaí had been confident that with Fiona Mitchell and Rachel Kirwan as star witnesses, Lawlor would have a lot of explaining to do. However, that was before Kirwan changed her story. In April 2019, when the trial date had been fixed, she walked back into Coolock Garda Station and said she'd lied when she told officers that Lawlor had issued threats against her or her boyfriend Derek Mitchell and said she only gave her original statements because

Fiona Mitchell had allegedly lied to her about DNA evidence. Her retraction was sure to cause a problem during the trial but still the officers hoped that Fiona's testimony and a sequence of events that had seen the Armed Support Unit scrambled even before the alert had been raised at the Mitchell house would convince a court of his guilt.

Lawlor's trial opened in the Central Criminal Court in early November, days after his brother-in-law Richie Carberry was shot dead at his home in Bettystown. Lawlor was livid and even more adamant than ever to beat the charges and win back his freedom so that he could avenge the murder. Lawlor listed his address as The Rise, Laytown, County Meath – his mother's home, where he had been staying on and off before he'd been taken into custody.

He stood to face the court, making sure he looked calm and respectable, as the charges were read to him. He pleaded not guilty to the attempted murder of Fiona Mitchell at Moatview Avenue in Priorswood, Dublin, on 26 May 2018. He pleaded not guilty to the charge of possession of a firearm with intent to endanger life at the same address and date. He pleaded not guilty to making a threat to Rachel Kirwan at Donaghmede at a date unknown between 1 and 31 January that year, and making a threat to kill or cause serious harm to Fiona and her son Derek Mitchell. And he also pleaded not guilty to shooting the German shepherd dog, Chopper, that night.

Opening the case, Mr John O'Kelly SC for the State told the jury of seven men and five women that of the five counts against Lawlor the most serious was the attempted murder of

Mrs Mitchell but that all five counts related to the same event. 'They are all part and parcel of something that started in January 2018,' he said. Mr O'Kelly told the court that Lawlor had been in a relationship with Rachel Kirwan for 12 years and that they had two children together, but they had split in the summer of 2017, and that Christmas Lawlor learned she was in a new relationship with Derek Mitchell. Mr O'Kelly said that was when Lawlor had begun a 'campaign of threats and intimidation', demanding she break up her new relationship, which culminated in the attempted murder of Mitchell's mother Fiona.

Addressing the jury and Mr Justice Paul McDermott, Mr O'Kelly said that Fiona Mitchell was getting ready for bed around one o'clock on the morning of 26 May when she heard her dog barking. When she looked out of her window she saw two men, one with a gun in his hand, who she recognised as Robbie Lawlor. The first shot fired, he said, shattered the patio door and Fiona Mitchell ran from the kitchen, locking the door behind her. When she was running up the hallway a second shot went off behind her, Mr O'Kelly told the court, adding that when gardaí arrived at the scene the two men had escaped. The officers went into the garden and found the dog dead. Fiona Mitchell immediately identified the gunman as Robbie Lawlor, he told the court, and told officers she had been receiving indirect threats from him over the previous months. Mr O'Kelly warned the jury that while the CCTV evidence gathered did not identify the gunman it did show two men going past another house towards Fiona Mitchell's home just before the attack and then getting away minutes later.

On 18 November Fiona Mitchell stood in the witness box, trying not to make eye contact with Robbie Lawlor as he stared at her intently. She told the court that Chopper had alerted her to intruders that night and when she looked out she first thought it was her neighbours' sons taking a shortcut home. She said she'd made toasted sandwiches and had given some to her younger son, who was in the sitting room. When she returned to the kitchen, Chopper's barking made her look out of the kitchen window. She said she saw Robert Lawlor dressed in black trousers and a black top facing her with a gun at her patio doors and with nothing covering his face. Guiding her evidence and anticipating every window of opportunity for the defence, Mr O'Kelly asked Fiona to describe the quality of her sight and she told him that it was a hundred per cent. He also asked her if she had any doubts who she was seeing and she'd answered 'None'. She went on to say that she knew it was Lawlor as she was constantly looking at photos of him on his Facebook and Instagram accounts. She said her son was in a relationship with Lawlor's ex-girlfriend, Rachel Kirwan, and that sometime around Christmas she was in a McDonald's restaurant at the Northside Shopping Centre with Derek when he'd got a phone call and she had overheard a threat from the man on the other end. This man, she said, told Derek: 'I am going to kill your ma; I will give you two weeks to grieve her and then I will come back and take you out of your misery.' Fiona told the court that she had started looking at his social media accounts after that.

Under cross-examination by Patrick McGrath SC, she was accused of becoming 'obsessed' with Lawlor prior to the shooting and 'stalking' him on the internet. Mitchell held firm, saying that she had only looked at photos of Lawlor so she could 'see who I'm dealing with, to see who is who'. She said she'd never messaged Lawlor and had never spoken to him. 'You were wrong to say that was him at the window,' Mr McGrath put to her, but she insisted: 'No, I'm not wrong.'

Under further cross-examination she was told that she had first said that two men in black were in her house and that she hadn't told the first garda she had dealt with about recognising Lawlor. Small discrepancies about where she was at the time the dog started barking were also put to her. 'You didn't see Robert Lawlor that night carrying out any incident at your house,' Mr McGrath concluded. Fiona responded, 'I did, I did see Robert Lawlor.'

As Fiona stepped down from the witness box she hoped she had done enough to convince the jury that she was telling the truth and that she knew Lawlor intimately as she was so terrorised by him. But she also knew that the jury had no idea about his background or the notorious reputation he enjoyed around Coolock, where he was the hitman everyone said had taken on Mr Big when he killed his friend Kenneth Finn. But whatever hopes Fiona had that she had done her best to convince the court of his guilt were dashed the following day when Rachel Kirwan sat into the witness box and started to weep. With her head in her hands Kirwan looked out from under waves of blonde hair and said that she had lied when she told gardaí that her former partner had threatened to kill her boyfriend and his mum. 'I made it up just to paint him in the worst light possible . . . I was lied to.'

Kirwan's change of heart couldn't have been more dramatic. Back in May 2018 when the incident had happened she'd given a statement to Sergeant Selina Proudfoot at Coolock Garda Station during which she described her relief when she drove to Fiona Mitchell's house and found her alive. In the stand Kirwan insisted that she had lied. She said that in April 2019 she had told gardaí that she had given incorrect accounts of the events because, she claimed, Fiona Mitchell had told her there was DNA evidence to prove that the man with the gun in her garden had been Lawlor. Although she had said in her statement that Lawlor had threatened to kill Derek Mitchell and his mother, she told the court that she had lied and that Lawlor had never made any such threat. During her evidence she even described the Mitchell house as a 'halfway house' and on the second day of her evidence, under cross-examination, described it as a 'party house, young fellas there morning, noon and night', adding, 'It's not a home, it's not a family home. The house was run like a business with drugs being sold.'

Later she repeatedly cried and held her head in her hands as Mr McGrath SC showed her four photographs of Derek Mitchell and asked her if she recognised anyone in them. 'I'm not answering questions about these photographs,' she told the court, but eventually identified Mitchell in all four. As the jury watched, Mr McGrath SC pointed to a second, taller man in the photos with Mitchell and asked Rachel Kirwan if she'd ever met him. She told the court she hadn't but she did know his name, adding, 'I don't feel comfortable saying his name.' But Mr McGrath pressed her: 'All I'm asking is for his name.' With dramatic effect

Kirwan paused before saying 'Kane Kirwan', who, she agreed, was also known as Kane McCormack.

McCormack Kirwan was a friend of Derek Mitchell who Lawlor had asked gardaí about when he was first arrested in relation to the gun attack. He'd thrown his name out to officers in a bid to cast doubt on his own involvement in the gun attack and point the investigation towards the Kinahan–Hutch feud instead. The Mitchells, Lawlor claimed, had allowed Kane to hide out at their home while he was under death threat from the Kinahan cartel.

McCormack Kirwan was a volatile 24-year-old whose father, Noel 'Duck Egg' Kirwan, had been killed on 26 December 2016 in a Kinahan-directed hit. 'Duck Egg' had been a lifelong friend of Gerry 'The Monk' Hutch and had attended the funeral of his brother Eddie, the first of a long line of Hutch family members and associates murdered in direct retaliation for the Regency Hotel attack. The motive for Kirwan's murder was ruthless but clear-cut and gardaí believed he was targeted because of his relationship with The Monk. When his son's body was discovered in a field in Clonee in County Meath a little over 13 months later things weren't a bit less clear. Kane had left his home and travelled to meet his killers before being shot three times and left to die. Kirwan had vocalised his desire to take revenge for his father's murder and gardaí had already foiled a previous attempt to assassinate him, but he knew people on both sides of the feud and was in contact with some of the most feared Kinahan loyalists, despite swearing vengeance against the mob.

While Lawlor knew that the Gardaí weren't going to drop him as a suspect and instead pursue a Kinahan angle in the shooting at the Mitchell home, he was clever enough to realise that it could cast some doubt in a future court case and that mentioning it under arrest meant it would have to be contained in the book of evidence against him.

Now, with his ex-girlfriend in the witness stand, his lawyers were focusing on the photographs showing Mitchell and McCormack Kirwan together. When asked who had downloaded the photographs from Mitchell's Instagram account, Rachel Kirwan refused to answer. 'I'm not answering that question. My life is worth more than four pictures on Instagram. I'm not answering anything more about who's in them pictures.' But Lawlor's counsel, Mr McGrath SC, said he was only interested in whether or not she had printed them out. Eventually she broke down crying as he continued: 'You printed these off in a chemist shop a week before this trial, didn't you? Were you in a chemist shop one week before this trial? It's a simple question. Do you remember a week before the trial? This is the last question I will ask you. Did you print these photos off from Mr Mitchell's Instagram account the week before the trial?' Despite his insistence, Rachel Kirwan continued to refuse to answer the question and was eventually stood down from the witness stand.

The following day two officers spoke of an encounter they had had with Robbie Lawlor hours before the gun attack. Detective Sergeant Noel Smith told the court that he'd been working with his colleague Garda Killian Leyden when he met Lawlor, dressed in black, at about 10.25 that night on the Strand Road near Inse Bay in Laytown. 'His behaviour was unusual. He was quite erratic,' he said. That had spurred the officers to call to his mother Celia Dillon's home. When they got there Lawlor was out, but on talking to his mother he believed that she too had concerns about her son's behaviour. When Lawlor got home the officer told the court: 'His behaviour was quite similar to what it was on the Strand Road and he became more aggressive in his stance towards myself and Garda Leyden.' According to the officer, when Lawlor's brother arrived back at the house, the gardaí left but drove around the area, where they bumped into Lawlor's stepfather, taxi driver Paul Dillon, as he made his way home. Detective Sergeant Smith told Dillon to inform him if he had any concerns and later that night Dillon called to say that Lawlor had left the house. The officer told the court that he was so concerned at that point that he contacted Rachel Kirwan before driving to Coolock Garda Station to brief two members of the Armed Support Unit (ASU). While he was there, he said, he'd received a phone call from Rachel Kirwan. 'She was screaming hysterically, "Get to Fiona's."' Detective Sergeant Smith said he'd told the ASU to get to Fiona Mitchell's home and that he had followed, finding her outside the front of the house. He described how she was 'hysterical' and shouted: 'They're in the house. They have guns.'

The ASU had entered the house with ballistic shields but found nobody inside and gave the all-clear. Detective Sergeant Smith said he went inside the house and noticed a hole in the kitchen door. He found Chopper dead in the garden. He told the jury that Fiona Mitchell told her at that point that Lawlor had fired two shots at her.

Another officer told the court about the arrest and interview of Lawlor in the aftermath of the attack. Detective Garda Brendan Mears said that he and Detective Garda Shay McGrath had interviewed Lawlor and quizzed him about his feelings around the relationship between his ex-partner and Derek Mitchell. He told the court that Lawlor had answered: 'I have no problem . . . She is my ex but I have a kid with another girl. Life goes on.'

He said that during the interview Lawlor had suggested a new line of inquiry for gardaí. 'He said that person who shot at the Mitchell home could have been the Hutches or the Kinahans. He said: "You haven't looked at that."' During the interview he described Fiona Mitchell as 'a fucking cunt' for naming him as the gunman. 'I don't know why she named me. She panicked. I was the first person to come into her head. She is a sick woman and a fucking liar. She has an obsession with me. She had been stalking me . . . Some crazy fool might want to shoot her but not me.' He told the officers that Derek Mitchell was fighting with the Kinahans and that he (Lawlor) didn't want his children in the Mitchell house. 'I warned him never to be around my kids but I'm not going to kill him over this. I said I wanted to meet with Mitchell . . . To lay down the laws as a father, as any man would.'

The court heard that Lawlor admitted he was in a difficult situation, having split with his former partner, but had asked: 'Was I in a murderous state? . . . Not enough to shoot a dog and shoot a woman . . . Everyone knows I am a good father but she has painted me as a mad murderer and a psychotic bastard. Maybe she is the one that needs help, not me . . . I have seen terrible things. I wouldn't lay a hand on a woman . . . I'm a great father and I'm a good bloke.'

On the final day of the trial Fiona Mitchell returned to the stand again and denied that Kane McCormack Kirwan had ever slept in her garden shed. Before the jury retired to consider their verdict they heard from each side once more. The State reiterated their case that it was Robbie Lawlor who fired a gun at Fiona Mitchell and killed her dog. Lawlor's defence said that he had played no role in the attack. Mr McGrath SC told the jury that they should reject the evidence given by Fiona Mitchell because she was 'neither reliable nor truthful'. Two hours and 40 minutes later the jury returned and told Justice Paul McDermott that they had found Robbie Lawlor not guilty on all five charges against him. In the dock he nodded his head and mouthed 'thank you' as the jury were discharged and thanked for their service. And just like that, on the afternoon of 9 December 2019 Lawlor was back on the streets, free to wreak more havoc. If Robbie Lawlor had been volatile before he was arrested for attempting to kill Fiona Mitchell, his mood had now hit stratospheric levels.

The news of Lawlor's release had immediately sparked huge Garda alerts. In Drogheda, Chief Superintendent Christy Mangan rallied his troops with the most up-to-date intelligence. Not only was Lawlor free, but Cornelius Price, one of his biggest gangland rivals, was also back in town. Price had been holed up in his compound in Gormanston after he'd been told of a plot to kill a close female relative. He'd been based between Manchester and Birmingham since the summer, having been released from Wheatfield Prison after completing a three-year sentence for reckless endangerment of a garda. To avoid attention Price had travelled home through Belfast via Scotland but two days after his return officers had been alerted that 'Nelly Boy' was back. Owen Maguire too was back home after signing himself out of hospital and had posted a social media video of himself winking at the cameras as he did pull-ups.

'When Robbie Lawlor was released we were made well aware of the fact that he would be out and about,' said Chief Superintendent Mangan:

> We were very much aware that he had had a falling-out with Cornelius Price in prison so when you have those strands of intelligence a clear picture emerges. We knew we would have a major problem and had to include him in our plans on a daily basis and every morning we would have carried out an assessment of what was taking place, what the temperature was within the criminal fraternity, coupled with dealing with the normal policing issues.

Mangan knew well what Robbie Lawlor was like and the effect his release was going to have on the already tense situation in his town.

> The minute Robbie Lawlor was in town there was a huge heightened anxiety amongst the criminals themselves, you could see the fear amongst them. They knew his history and what he was capable of doing and that he would try and do it in Drogheda, so there was a major panic between all of the groupings and even though he was working with the younger

group they were very much afraid of him too because he was likely to turn around and kill one of them and that is the sort of character you were dealing with, someone who could be pretty charismatic one day and then in the afternoon pull out a gun and shoot you; somebody who could engage and be very intelligent but then in that conversation he is having with you he is making a decision to kill you. Thankfully, he is not the sort of a person that you meet every day or that you will see too often but there are some capable of that. That is their DNA. Of course at that point he is laying the blame for the murder of his brother-in-law, Richie Carberry, firmly at the feet of a number of characters; Cornelius Price, Owen Maguire and Mr Big.

Back in Coolock, Mr Big had been living up to his name and reputation and despite being only in his early forties was looked upon as a gangland veteran, a capo dei capi of sorts. He'd come up the hard way under the tutelage of a notorious criminal, Pascal Kelly, a master burglar and tiger kidnapper who'd survived a number of assassination attempts during the 1990s. Kelly had ridden the crest of the drugs wave using funds he'd raised in violent and terrifying robberies to buy shipments and place himself at the top of the pile. Kelly was a bully and he'd ordered Mr Big and other young gang members about. He'd moved out of Dublin and into a hilltop home in Cavan which sat on three-quarters of an acre and where he had built stables. Inside he'd fitted a Jacuzzi and a bar and had a collection of expensive cars parked up on the driveway. But when his carefully constructed empire began to unravel around 2014, Mr Big had smelled blood and weakness. Kelly had been targeted by CAB and, under pressure, had messed up a post office robbery in 2014 which had netted just €92,000 for the gang. Kelly and two others had burst into a house in Malahide, tying up a postmistress, her daughter and an Italian student with cable ties and holding them in a field overnight before bringing the woman to her workplace and stealing the money. Kelly had been sloppy and left behind evidence and DNA and with two convictions for robbery (from 1997 and 1989) faced a hefty jail sentence if found guilty. The pressure had got to him and with the attention of the CAB on his home and assets he'd snapped, threatening an officer. Facing that offence, along with tiger kidnap charges, and failure to provide tax returns, he'd become desperate for money and when he fell out with his underling, Mr Big, he'd been forced to flee the country, returning under an assumed identity and hiding out in a rented one-bed holiday home, where he was eventually nabbed by gardaí.

Facing down the likes of Pascal Kelly did nothing to harm Mr Big's own reputation, but it wasn't the only reason he had become feared and revered in equal measure – after all, he'd coolly murdered rivals and traitors and beaten the criminal justice system himself a number of times. Despite the 2009 introduction of the new gangland legislation that allowed gardaí bring organised crime members before the Special Criminal Court, it had taken almost a decade for the system to get up to speed with the new offences. In the intervening period, as the Gardaí tested the legislation and the Director of Public Prosecutions trod carefully, a number of high-profile criminals had got lucky and found themselves before a jury in the Circuit Courts. Mr Big had been charged in relation to a high-profile robbery that had taken place in the years immediately after 2009. The case received a lot of media attention. Mr Big had strict bail conditions and was regularly photographed as he arrived at Garda stations to sign on, looking fresh and fit. He exuded an air of confidence and respectability, showing up to court dressed more like a young tech executive than a gangland criminal. He'd fobbed off belief evidence from gardaí that he was one of the biggest criminals in the country and evaded comments about his fortified home. (Belief evidence is evidence accepted by the courts as the belief of senior-ranking gardaí as to the status of particular criminals and their activities.) The first trial collapsed amid suspicions of jury intimidation; the second was set aside when the Director of Public Prosecutions dropped the charges. Mr Big had also got lucky in the North, where he had faced trial for money-laundering and had spent a period of time in custody before the charges were dropped.

Unlike some who pleaded guilty to get a lesser sentence, Mr Big preferred to play Russian roulette and take his chances by denying anything put to him by the State. His confident air as he walked to and from courts, his ability to beat the system and his reputation as a ruthless killer made him an icon of sorts in gangland and he found an army of ambitious young soldiers happy to work under his command. Theirs was a different generation from his own and the old-school path to crime through armed robbery and street dealing, which he had taken, no longer existed. In Mr Big's day, gang members like himself were usually in their late twenties before they gained any importance at all. But the cocaine boom had changed everything. Where once aspiring young criminals at the bottom of the food chain started out joyriding or with petty crime, no such apprenticeships now existed. Within his own community, Mr Big had found countless young men willing to move straight into debt collection and extreme violence when they were still just teenagers. Many were the children of his own contemporaries or those whose upbringing had been blighted by organised crime. Mr Big was happy to use young men to do his bidding, particularly as his own profile rose and he became subject to ongoing Garda surveillance. The young men were handy and allowed him to control his patch at arm's length. In 2016 he had got some of his teen criminals to burn a gym, believing it was going to take away business from another gym he controlled. Gardaí had some successes against him – in 2018 a €3 million haul of ketamine and MDMA (ecstasy) was seized in a joint operation between the Gardaí and Revenue – but he had become very rich and powerful, in particular because of the cunning he had developed into a business.

Above all, it was feuding that suited Mr Big as it had drawn the attention and the resources of the force away from him, particularly as localised gangs had gone to war. While Mr Big groomed his own army of youngsters, the Gardaí were firefighting an explosion of violence which had come about as a direct result of the dismantling of the Kinahan structure. Fuelled by a crack cocaine epidemic, Darndale and Coolock had become the epicentre of a new drug war that resulted in multiple deaths. There were many feuds in his own area. While the massive attention on the Kinahan–Hutch feud and even the Drogheda gang wars had drawn on a finite budget of law enforcement, it had also allowed Mr Big sit back and consider the playing pitch. At war, each gang had been forced to show their hand with competent killers and enforcers as well as allegiances with other groupings. Like a board game, each grouping came to the table with their big pieces and it was easy to discern which losses would unbalance their power. Mr Big himself had significant players in his ranks and even among the hot-headed youngsters he knew how to identify those who would be of use to him in battles to come. It was among that new world order that he had found the perfect soldier with a penchant for violence and a deep-seated hatred of Robbie Lawlor, his sworn enemy who had murdered his own secret weapon and close friend, Kenneth Finn.

CHAPTER SIX

The Gym Bag

It starts with shaky footage and a close-up of a black parka jacket with lots of voices shouting at one another. Quickly the face of Robbie Lawlor, the man in the jacket, comes into frame. He is surrounded but not worried. 'I'll tell ya what we'll do,' he starts to shout at the crowd jostling him. Quickly he is pushed backwards by a forceful shove and struggles to keep his footing on the pavement. The strap of a gym bag is wrapped around his shoulder but he takes the bag off and starts to lurch at some of the young men while another shouts: 'That's only the start of it! That's only the start of it! That is only the start of it, Robbie!' With that, Lawlor retreats, leaving his bag behind, and laughs manically at his attackers as the video flickers off. Days later the video goes viral, shared across WhatsApp and later on YouTube. It's December 2019 and Robbie Lawlor is enjoying his first weeks of freedom.

Unlike most criminals, whose exit from the prison system is an uneventful affair, Lawlor's freedom had sparked a major security alert across the country. After winking and mouthing 'thank you' to the jury at the Circuit Court who'd found him not guilty of the attempted murder of Fiona Mitchell and of threatening her son Derek, Lawlor had pulled on a parka jacket, zipped it up over his grey suit, pulled up the hood and walked determinedly out into a freezing December Monday in Dublin. Across the city, north to Drogheda and on the desks of every major specialist unit, a warning notice had been issued for all gardaí to be alert to Lawlor's presence and to approach him with caution should a situation arise. His elevated status meant that anywhere he was seen or suspected to be, the company he kept and his movements were to be closely monitored and fed into the system. While Fiona Mitchell felt hugely exposed, having given evidence against him in court, she wasn't the first in line for his twisted revenge. Instead Lawlor had clear targets in his head and none of them related to his domestic strife. He was plotting to carry out a one-man crime wave, to murder his three top rivals: Cornelius Price, Owen Maguire and Mr Big.

Days after Lawlor's release he was spotted in Drogheda and in the run-up to Christmas, to make the task of policing the town even more fraught, Price returned from the UK and bedded down in his compound in Gormanston. Intelligence suggested that Price had returned because he'd been informed that Lawlor was planning to murder a female companion who had remained there. Price had been moving between Manchester and Birmingham since his own release from Wheatfield Prison that summer, where he'd served a three-year sentence for the reckless endangerment of a garda. He'd left the UK after the attempted murder of one of the younger crew in the anti-Price–Maguire faction and had travelled home via Scotland and Belfast. He'd already been in Ireland two days before it was known that he'd returned. In the meantime, the video of a defiant Maguire doing pull-ups and winking at the camera had popped up on social media. There was no doubt that the battle lines were being drawn. Such was the animosity between the main protagonists that it was clear that blood would be spilled, and all that was before the gym bag incident.

What followed in the immediate aftermath of the video of Lawlor being attacked outside his gym was series of images of his young rivals posting photos of themselves wearing the black and white flip-flops that had been in the bag they'd snatched. The photos were accompanied by mocking notes taunting Lawlor about Carberry and cryptic messages about his own alleged victims, including David 'Fred' Lynch. Since March 2009, Lawlor had been suspected of shooting Lynch four times in the head with a handgun. The 26-year-old's body had been found on a patch of wasteland off Belcamp Lane in Coolock, but despite the best efforts of investigators Lawlor had never been charged, and getting away with the Lynch murder had become a badge he'd worn with pride. Dublin is often described as a small city and in a measure of how tiny its gangland really is, gardaí suspected that one of the youths outside the gym who'd videoed the gym bag scenes was a young lieutenant of Mr Big and one of his army of enforcers and debt collectors who was also a close associate of Lynch. Such was the young man's loyalty to the memory of Lynch that throughout his teenage years he'd vowed that he'd eventually get even with Lynch's killer, no matter how long he had to wait. Christmas came and went, Garda leave was cancelled in Drogheda, a town by now on a knife edge, and at the Carberry home in Bettystown a family in mourning gathered for the first festive season without a dad and beloved husband. Within weeks another family would know just what it was like to suffer a violent bereavement.

On the afternoon of 13 January 2020 the sister of a teenager called Keane Mulready-Woods, Courtney, put out an appeal on her Facebook account for anyone who might have seen him in the previous 24 hours. 'Has anyone seen my brother, he's only 17 and he's missing since yesterday evening and no one heard from him or can get through to him and anyone he's usually with is texting me looking for him.' Keane had been warned by gardaí in Drogheda that his life was under threat eight days before, on 5 January, so the situation was critical. The last time his family had heard from him was the day before the Facebook posting, when he rang his mother Bernadette. The last reported sighting of him was at about 6pm on the same day, on St Dominic's Bridge in Drogheda. Mulready-Woods was no saint; he'd mixed with bad company after dropping out of school early and had become involved in petty offending in his mid-teens, lured by the promise of money, designer clothes and prestige. His descent into the criminal underworld happened faster than usual, largely due to the job opportunities that were available in the town resulting from the simmering feud and the split in the Maguire organisation. He had quickly become bedded in with drug gangs when the feuds began to heat up.

Right: Alan Ryan, the head of the Real IRA in Dublin, who was murdered in 2012.

Below: Retired Chief Superintendent Christy Mangan who headed up the Drogheda feud investigation.

Cornelius Price, who headed up one side of the Drogheda feud before his death in 2023.

Daniel Kinahan, head of the Kinahan Organised Crime Group.

Derek 'Maradonna' Dunne, a former League of Ireland soccer player turned heroin dealer who was murdered in Amsterdam in 2000.

Eamon 'The Don' Dunne, a major figure in organised crime who was shot dead in 2010.

John Gilligan, whose gang murdered journalist Veronica Guerin.

Joseph and Helen Maughan with a picture of their son William Maughan and his girlfriend Ana Varslavane. Both are missing, presumed murdered.

Seventeen-year-old Keane Mulready Woods who was murdered and dismembered by Robbie Lawlor.

Larry Dunne, Ireland's first drug kingpin.

Martin Cahill, a legendary Irish criminal whose life story has been reflected in the movie *The General*.

Warren Crossan, a dissident Republican who was quizzed about the murder of Robbie Lawlor, and was then shot dead in Belfast in 2021.

Robbie Lawlor, the hitman who was shot dead in April 2020 in Ardoyne, Belfast.

The house at Etna Drive where Robbie Lawlor was shot dead.

Right: Wayne Dundon, serving a life sentence for the murder of Roy Collins in Limerick.

Below: Couple Ana Varslavane and William Maughan who disappeared in April 2015 from Gormanstown area of County Meath. Both are presumed murdered.

Keane's parents were separated and his father Barry would later be named in an affidavit filed with the High Court as part of a CAB case against Owen Maguire and his brother Brendan. In the affidavit a complaint made by Barry Woods over an attack on his car was listed to highlight dozens of incidents involving the gang's involvement in serious criminality. Keane was just 14 when he first came to the attention of youth workers and officers when he was accused of assaulting another boy. By 15 he was listed as an associate of the Price–Maguire organisation and had allegedly pointed a gun at a manager of a shop, an incident caught on CCTV but for which he was never prosecuted. Keane had begun his fledgling career carrying out petrol and pipe bomb attacks on the gang's rivals and their family members. His role was to threaten and intimidate those who owed debts. A year before his disappearance he'd smashed the window of the home of the mother of a boy who owed money before lobbing a petrol bomb through her window. He was convicted, given a four-month suspended sentence and placed on curfew. He was later caught with a small amount of cannabis. While his path to a career in criminality was clear, the infamy he would gain that January could never have been predicted. The fact was that in just a few days the underworld of organised crime had set a new unimaginable precedent in depravity that reflected the narco terrorists of Colombia and Mexico. Young Keane would be at the very centre of it.

Twenty-four hours after the Facebook post seeking help to locate Keane, body parts were discovered in a bag in the Moatview Drive estate in Coolock, in the heartland of the Mr Big organisation and where many of the youths who had attacked

Robbie Lawlor outside the gym lived. The discovery was made by a father of two who noticed the bag on the side of the road, picked it up and brought it to his house before examining the contents. He would later give an anonymous interview describing how he heard police sirens and suspected that the bag was filled with drugs or stolen goods. When he opened it he thought it contained animal meat before realising that what he was looking at was a human leg. The man panicked and put the bag back where he had picked it up, and in the commotion neighbours were alerted and called the gardaí. When officers first arrived they appeared dismissive, but when they looked in the bag they realised that it contained severed limbs. The bag was a black Puma sports bag and in it were Keane Mulready-Woods, legs along with a pair of black and white flip-flops.

That evening in Drogheda John Myles had picked up two passengers in his taxi. Unknown to him, in the front seat was Paul Crosby, the man who'd phoned Owen Maguire to taunt him about nappies and wheelchairs. At about 6.20, just metres from the Garda station at the Bridge of Peace, a vehicle cut him off, two masked men jumped out and started to point at his vehicle. Despite the traffic all around the gunmen started to fire and the two passengers jumped out and fled. Mr Myles, who'd been working as a taxi man for ten years, was shot in the back. He'd later describe his terror on the Michael Reade show on the local LMFM radio station:

> The bullet went in and out, luckily enough it didn't lodge in the back, but if it had gone further I would have been paralysed

for the rest of my life . . . If I hadn't turned I would have been killed, my kids would have been planning my funeral. I done nothing wrong on anybody. I picked up a lad and I ended up getting shot while he got out like the coward he is and ran . . . I don't want to know who done it, I don't care who done it. They were pointing at him, he was getting out and that was it, because he scoured out across me and ran, it was me who got it because I couldn't get my seat belt off quick enough . . . He got out across me, don't know how he did it, the girl got out the back side of the car, and the two of them ran and left me there. Whether I was dead or alive, they didn't care. I could have bled to death - they do what they do because they can't do an honest day's work and we all have to suffer because of what they're doing. It's us that has to suffer . . . It's me that's shot, it's me that's suffering and has to explain to my kids what happened and how it happened. My daughter won't go to school now, she's at home. Because she's panicking, so what do you do after that? Where do you go after that? These people think they can do what they like, when they like to people and my natural reaction by turning saved my life yesterday. I'm sitting here today because of that. They thought they were free to go along and shoot someone who had nothing to do with them. I want to clear my name as well - I can prove that I didn't do anything wrong, I picked up a fare, done my work and got shot.

The taxi driver said that many people would not go into certain areas of Drogheda because of the ongoing feud and admitted that he hesitated when picking up the fare. 'I thought I'd pick him up, it will be a one-off. I'll take a chance. I was thinking what's going to happen? It's too busy. I didn't know he was being watched getting into my car – I went one route. Because they were watching him I'm where I am today – the car in the garage and me shot.'

In Drogheda station all hands were on deck. At the same time Keane Mulready-Woods was being reported missing the day before, intelligence was coming in through a network of informants that he was already dead. The shooting, which had clearly happened in retaliation, was exactly the type of response officers had feared. Mangan knew that this was the most serious development in the feud to date and he also knew that Robbie Lawlor was responsible for one of the most gruesome crimes Ireland would ever see. He'd later recall:

> Robbie Lawlor is in Drogheda the night that Keane Mulready-Woods goes missing and he is sighted around Drogheda and on the Monday, 13 January. Keane is reported missing almost at the same time that we are receiving reports that he is dead and has been killed. That night body parts are found in Coolock. They had been thrown out of a car in a holdall with a pair of sliders, they are gym shoes. So they were positioned with the body parts. Robbie had had a row with [some] young people during which his gym bag was stolen and he was being taunted about that. The message is 'this is what can happen to you if you mess with me.'

Gardaí were not only privy to the fact that Mulready-Woods was dead even before DNA examinations could be carried out on the remains in the sports bag, they had also been told about where and when he had met his grisly end. 'From an early stage we could identify where the crime scene had been, where he had been killed and his body dismembered,' said Mangan. Searches were conducted in the Rathmullan Park area, one of the council estates that had been central to feud activity for years. There, a house was quickly sealed off and crime scene investigators started arriving in their droves. The house belonged to Gerard 'Ged' McKenna, a father of eight who had long-term difficulties with drink and drugs. As teams started to examine the house and yard more remains showed up in dramatic circumstances in Dublin. Locals saw a burning car at Trinity Terrace in Drumcondra, believing it to be a stolen car which had been set ablaze by joyriders. When they responded to the 999 call, at 1.30am, Dublin Fire Brigade personnel found a smouldering head in the boot. Mangan recalled:

> The remains were in a Volvo found burnt out and more parts of Keane Mulready-Woods remains are found in that car. The torso is still missing and we believe it is being held and it was going to be put at the compound in Gormanston in an attempt to frighten Cornelius Price. That was the warped logic. So you are dealing with a very sensitive murder investigation.

Mangan, in charge of the response to the murder of Keane Mulready-Woods, which was already making headlines around the world, knew that he had one opportunity to set the narrative in appeals for information. The press conference to be held less than 24 hours after the burning car was found would be vital in setting the tone for the months to come. Mangan knew it would be very important to make sure that the public did not think that Keane Mulready-Woods was just another gang member with skin in the game, one who lived by the gun and therefore died by the gun.

> From the start we really emphasised that Keane Mulready-Woods was a child and that he had got caught up between the warring factions, an impressionable young person. He was a boy trying to make his way in life. He wasn't unlike a lot of other young people all over Dublin, and every major town in Ireland, where they become involved in criminal activity and then grow out of it. And they do, the majority do, actually. It is only a small minority that will continue into their twenties and thirties and serve long prison sentences. So there was every possibility that Keane could have got through this, but I suppose an indication of the level of his involvement was that he had a ballistic vest. At 17 years of age to believe that you need to wear a bulletproof vest says a lot and he obviously felt under a certain level of threat himself. His death, because I was in Drogheda that night, caused an air of despondency. People were terrified. I was receiving a lot of calls that night from people who were really, really afraid. They thought the town was going to descend into total chaos. And it was my job to make sure that didn't happen. You are there to keep people safe. We set up the investigation and like in any of the major ones I used the media in a way to get the message out there – that a child had died. Media will always seek out information and they are very useful to you. The message was

Keane Mulready-Woods was a child and we weren't going to let this sit. The investigation would bring the people in charge to justice.

Also announced at the press conference was the forensic examination results that the limbs in the bag in Coolock were positively those of Keane Mulready-Woods. His sister again took to Facebook to express her grief. 'You are so special in my life that I know no other person will be able to take your place my brother,' Courtney said. Independent councillor John Lyons said: 'There is a feeling that there would be more done if this was happening in Castleknock and not Coolock. There have been four murders all only minutes' walk from where this happened. People are fearful, they are rightly fearful and keeping their heads down. But sadly people are not surprised.'

Mangan recalls:

When we confirmed that the remains that had been found in Dublin were Keane Mulready-Woods, it's for me ... well ... it was unfathomable. Everyone was shocked and it takes a lot to shock someone around as long as I had been. I'd worked in An Garda Síochána for forty years and unfortunately I'd seen a lot of bad things happen. To try to comprehend that someone would inveigle a child into a house and then proceed to kill them and dismember their body and simply discard it then in a number of locations was absolutely shocking. Yeah, it was shocking. The people of Drogheda were very shocked. But ultimately it was a reality check – time to regain control. Because control is almost lost at that point, it is within fingertips of being lost and . . . criminals would have almost taken over a town. And I think for me I couldn't allow that to happen. You do have a reserve of energy and ability and need to decide how we are going to take this crew out and take them down.

The remains of Keane Mulready-Woods were taken to the city morgue. Behind the scenes gardaí had wasted no time identifying the two main suspects – Robbie Lawlor and Paul Crosby – but they couldn't show their hand in case it would negate any useful witness information coming in from the public. They knew it was vital to encourage anyone who had seen anything to come forward and to reiterate that a child had been killed, caught up in a greedy, bloody underworld cocaine feud between two rival gangs. A description of the clothing Keane Mulready-Woods was wearing when he disappeared completed the picture of a youth who had been drawn to the lure of the money involved in the drug business: navy Hugo Boss tracksuit bottom, black Hugo Boss trainers with brown soles and black laces, a red and orange Canada Goose jacket valued at over €800, and a Gucci baseball cap costing around €350. Garda Deputy Commissioner, Policing and Security John Twomey said:

> An Garda Síochána is determined to bring those behind this shocking crime to justice. In recent years An Garda Síochána has made significant progress in tackling organised crime through arrests leading to convictions and major seizures of guns, drugs and cash. This focus will continue. As always, the help and support of communities is vital to this.

Information or dashcam footage from anyone in the Moatview Drive/Moatview Gardens, Dublin 17 area on Monday 13 January from 9 to 10pm was sought, along with information on the movements of the blue Volvo S40 bearing false registration plates 141 MO 1925, which was abandoned and set on fire in the Trinity Terrace, Dublin 3 area. The car had been taken from a premises in Sandymount in County Dublin a month earlier, on 15 December 2019.

Forensic examinations continued at the house at Rathmullan Park, while political calls for extra gardaí grew. Days after the discovery, Garda Commissioner Drew Harris visited Drogheda and Coolock Garda stations and assured senior officers of his support.

Three days after the first Facebook posting, images started to appear online and were shared among WhatsApp groups. They showed the inside of a house and grotesque, barbaric images of severed limbs and a chainsaw. The video was clear enough to make out sinews of muscle and flesh, severed bones and evidence of blood. The homemade movie had no sound and the silence made it all the more sinister. In quick succession another video went up, this time of a man, dressed in a balaclava, threatening to kill Robbie Lawlor. Officers asked people not to share the online content but the macabre interest of the public meant that the images were shared thousands of times.

Politicians came out in force. Taoiseach Leo Varadkar promised to visit Drogheda and addressed the residents of Rathmullan Park directly, saying it was 'the most gruesome, grotesque murder I can think of'. Local politician Ged Nash, writing in the *Irish Mirror*, said:

The horrific murder and dismemberment of Keane Mulready-Woods has seen the crossing of a threshold in Irish society. The people of Drogheda and the people of Ireland are sickened to the core ... The heinous act represents a new and disgusting low. It demands a response from the government and authorities the likes of which we have never witnessed before. It's not the innocent families of Drogheda who should be lying awake at night, sick with worry about who might be next, it is the gangsters involved in this deadly feud who should be kept from their sleep fearing the knock on the door from the Gardaí. This feud has gone too far ... We need our dedicated local gardaí to be supported by a massive 'Limerick style' policing and criminal justice system ... I love my town. We are all proud of who we are and where we are from. This small bunch of people intent on wiping each other out do not represent us.

In a throwback to far long-gone times when terrorists and gangsters often accepted the intervention of the clergy, a priest offered to mediate. Fr Conor McGee said the brutal murder revealed a 'new level of ferociousness'. Bishop Michael Router, the Auxiliary Bishop of Armagh, who lived in County Louth and who had spoken out about the murder of Keith Brannigan, said:

> The murder of Keane has taken violence to such a point that enough is enough. The gangs are grooming children and society needs to take back control so vulnerable children can be cherished and not exploited. There are people with blood on their hands and we all have a responsibility to assist the

Gardaí to apprehend not just the perpetrator of this evil, but also the gang leaders who orchestrated it.

On 17 January a number of things happened; one in particular would be a turning point for Mangan's team, and on that day his calls for extra resources would be properly heard. Early that morning the British rapper Bugzy Malone weighed in to the sensational media story about Keane and paid tribute to his murdered teenage fan. The Manchester star posted a photo of the pair together with the comment, 'I've just had some bad news that one of my young fans has passed away. Keane Mulready-Woods, I just want to send my regards out to his family and friends. Gutted, I hope the family is OK, rest in peace.' The posting was quickly passed around Keane's teenage friends, who saw it as a measure of his impact on the world. What they didn't see was the attention being given to his death politically. That morning Taoiseach Leo Varadkar visited the town and issued a fighting response to the out-of-control gangland players who had focused global attention on Drogheda. While gardaí recovered bloody machetes used in the teenager's killing and found remnants of clothing in a makeshift fire at the back of the Rathmullan Park house crime scene, Varadkar, along with Minister for Justice Charlie Flanagan and his deputy, Fergus O'Dowd, made a political show of strength in the affected areas before they went for a special briefing prepared by Mangan at the Garda HQ. The Taoiseach said:

> We're in Drogheda today and first of all I'd like to express my revulsion and condemnation of the very serious crime that has taken place here and also to assure the people of Drogheda that

the government is one hundred per cent behind them. We are going to get these people behind bars, we are going to make this town safe again. After this I'm going to the Garda station for a briefing and to find out from them if there's anything else we can do, if there is any more support for their efforts. I really want to say to people across the country and also people here in Drogheda, that crime doesn't pay, that we will get these people behind bars and make this town safe again. And I really want to encourage anyone that has evidence or information to come forward, because to get people into the Special Criminal Court, to get them convicted, we need evidence, the Gardaí need information and people who bring that evidence forward or agree to become witnesses will be protected.

Mangan had been up all night preparing to brief the Taoiseach. He needed people and support to a degree that Drogheda had never seen, and he needed to convince the powers that be that, for the first time since Limerick's feuds, an area outside the capital needed to be flooded with gardaí.

Up to that point, I would consider we were very much on our own. I had a certain amount of officers to deal with this and I could get a sense from the officers, when we were having a conference in relation to whatever crime we were investigating, I could see their driven commitment that they were willing to be there twenty-four seven. But we needed help and that help eventually came, but it took the death of Keane Mulready-Woods for that to happen. And then we got a huge injection of personnel. The appointment I had in Drogheda a couple of days after the murder with the Taoiseach Leo Varadkar was very important. I knew he only had a certain number of minutes to give and was coming to meet us and get a sense of what was going on. I thought he would only be there for half an hour or forty-five minutes and I had a presentation ready of a number of serious crimes. One thing I showed him was a video of the incident where a man was shot twice – in it you can see that the gunman, as he is shooting, barely missed a woman walking along, literally less than a foot from her back. She was an innocent bystander who could have been killed. Varadkar was visibly shocked and he was due to go but, to be fair, he stayed for over another hour and we went into a discussion about the root cause of it all, which was criminality, but also cocaine. We had a very detailed discussion and I clearly said to him that at that time we had a tsunami of cocaine in the country. I said it was so readily available, no matter what town, village or hamlet, you can get your bag and that is the root cause of this dispute. I got huge resources after that.

Ironically, at the exact time the Taoiseach was being briefed on the effects of cocaine on communities and the emergency situation that had developed in Drogheda, another out-of-control criminal was carrying on regardless in Dublin. Businessman Barry Wolverson had just pulled into his scrapyard premises at Madigan's Yard in Swords when he was shot by Bernard Fogarty and Robert 'Roo' Redmond. With more than fifty previous convictions, Fogarty had spent the previous ten months developing an online career as a gangland influencer, posting crazed videos as he cruised the streets of Coolock looking for targets and calling them out. His videos included footage of him pulling out a knife, calling out rivals and waving wads of €50 notes and offering rewards for information on his enemy. In one he had threatened to attack one of two Coolock brothers, saying: 'You have one more day to come out and fight me like a fucking man. Fucking faggot. One more day. If you don't come out and start fighting, watch, other people are going to start falling victim you fucking rat . . . Fucking come out and fucking fight.' He then played a music video with the lyrics, 'I've got murder on my mind'. Fogarty, then 35, had worked as a Kinahan gunman and had been arrested just months earlier after shooting Mark Ivers in Donaghmede. Along with Redmond, who had amassed more than 90 previous convictions, the pair had launched a two-man crime wave in their bid to collect debts and fund the lifestyle and luxury items that Fogarty regularly displayed in his videos. Redmond had left voice messages from his own phone threatening those he said owed him money, and even their mothers. On one occasion he had travelled to Tyrone and shot through the windows of a family home after claiming he was owed more than €250,000 by a son who wasn't even living at the house. He had ordered the shooting of Jordan Davis, who, he claimed, owed him €70,000, hiring gunman Wayne Cooney to take on the job. Davis had been pushing his four-month-old son in a buggy in a laneway beside Our Lady Immaculate national school in Darndale on 22 May 2019 when he was killed.

The shooting of Wolverson was the pair's last act of violence and would see them finally taken off the streets and placed in custody. Officers from Coolock arrested Fogarty and Redmond around 12.25pm, noticing a smell of petrol from Fogarty's tracksuit bottoms and seeing that he had a lighter in his hand. Just 300 yards away at Greenwood estate they had managed to get under control a smouldering Citroën C4 which had been set alight with two fire logs. A third fire log was found in the back of Fogarty's car. Later, at Coolock Garda Station, while under arrest and before forensic testing could be done, Fogarty attempted to wash his hands with Lynx shower gel. Firearms residue would be discovered on his and Redmond's hoodies. Wolverson lived but never regained consciousness. His life support system was shut off more than a year later. During the murder trial that followed a court would hear that Fogarty and Redmond had been observed on CCTV moving in tandem on the morning of the shooting and in the Citroën at the yard earlier in the morning, and later as Barry Wolverson drove into it before midday. Both had been caught on CCTV a number of times and near the burnt-out car in Greenwood estate. The day before, Fogarty had been filmed purchasing three fire logs from a Circle K petrol station.

In Drogheda the man at the centre of the biggest murder hunt in the history of the criminal underworld was carrying on regardless. Just like Fogarty and Redmond, such was his disconnect from ordered society that one day just merged into the next, no matter what was happening on the political or policing front. For those on the front line who might encounter Lawlor in this state of mind it was of prime importance to know what to do and how to handle him. Mangan explains:

Robbie's modus operandi was completely different to anyone else. It was almost impossible to predict what he was going to do. He didn't align himself to very many people, he wouldn't impart too much information to potential informants who would let us know what was going to happen, or be about to happen. He was very much a maverick. He would decide that he was going to kill somebody and then he would go and do it and he would do it himself. He wouldn't be looking for a gunman to come in from the UK or Northern Ireland or anywhere else. He would simply go and do it himself.

Detectives had established a number of things, one being that the maverick attitude that set Robbie apart from his contemporaries meant that he wouldn't be hiding from anyone before or after the murder. Lawlor had been spotted in Drogheda on the night Keane Mulready-Woods had gone missing and he was also seen in the town on the Monday evening when the body parts were discovered in the sports bag in Coolock. As Mangan explained,

Lawlor didn't go to ground immediately. He was in the Drogheda area the night of the murder and the next day. He didn't go running. He is out and about, the man about town. Both before and after he had been up in Dublin and flitting up and down the North. He doesn't go into hiding at all. A number of other people did go into hiding believing that they were going to be next, in particular a number of the younger people, who would have been aged 17 and 18, and there were a number very fearful that they would be next and killed in similar fashion to Keane Mulready-Woods. Locally people were keeping their heads down but not the main protagonists.

With such heightened tension, attention had to briefly focus on the young Garda recruits who had come out of Templemore training college and straight into the war zone that was Drogheda. Mangan and his senior team wanted no casualties, so they had to give the unarmed newbies the psychological tools to fight the gangsters.

> Everyone had to get up and get going really quickly. The young gardaí coming out of Templemore had made a massive contribution to helping solve the issue, but we had to impart our experience to them. We would sit down on a daily basis with the units starting to work in the morning and we would tell them what was happening and how they were to deal with the different groupings for their own personal safety because they weren't armed. The younger people had to learn to 'speed deal' with some of the more volatile criminals in the country, some of the most dangerous I have ever met. Specific advice came around when stopping a car to make sure they were safe. A normal stop of a car is an easy and pleasant enough exercise, maybe not for the person you are stopping but for the garda. It's an everyday occurrence. We had to advise the recruits how to deal with criminals when stopping them so they didn't get hit by a car or that they would pull a gun or a knife out because they were actively transporting drugs, pipe bombs, guns, all over. There was an emphasis about their own personal safety. They were told when coming to work to make sure there was no one doing surveillance and when going home that there was nobody following them. They were given crash courses in anti-surveillance tactics and all

that kind of stuff was emphasised on a daily basis for their own personal safety. They were told to make sure that they were not going to be on their own as they might be targeted. The last thing I wanted was for a young garda walking into Robbie Lawlor in his prime and they might not know how to handle themselves or deal with him.

In the incident room gardaí needed to focus on what they knew, and they did know a number of things. First, Keane Mulready-Woods appeared to have been playing both sides in the feud, and while his father was a member of the Price–Maguire faction and he'd been known to collect debts on their behalf, witnesses had said he looked comfortable the night he went missing, the evening he'd agreed to meet with Paul Crosby outside a Centra shop in the Ballsgrove area of Drogheda town. Despite being paranoid enough to wear a ballistic vest he'd showed up in a taxi and had greeted Crosby like an old friend. The two had gone into the shop together and then after coming out got into a Volkswagen car being driven by Gerard 'Rocky' Cruise. Cruise appeared to have driven them to the laneway at the back of the Rathmullan Park home belonging to Gerard 'Ged' McKenna. Witnesses had said they'd last seen him there at 6.48pm on the night he went missing in the company of three men, one fitting the description of Robbie Lawlor. Second, officers knew that the kill would likely only satisfy Lawlor for a brief period. Like a serial killer, he would take a 'down period' in the aftermath of the murder of Mulready-Woods but such was his unpredictability it would be hard to estimate how long it would take him to kill again. And third, the murder was sure to make Lawlor a more prized target than ever for his rivals. First in the queue would surely be Owen Maguire, facing a lifetime in a wheelchair after Lawlor had tried to kill him. Second in line would be his formerly loyal right-hand man, the violent Cornelius Price, whose prison showdown with Lawlor meant the pair were locked in a fight to the death situation. Third was the wily criminal Mr Big who'd lost both a best friend and prized hitman at Lawlor's hands when he'd shot dead Kenneth Finn in what he believed was a strategic move ordered by the late Richie Carberry. And that wasn't counting the countless enemies that Lawlor had made in his short and volatile lifetime in which he'd constantly fallen out with friends and foes alike. Lawlor might have been the Garda's most wanted man but he was also living on borrowed time as his gangland enemies circled and unlikely underworld allegiances began to form into a complex web of betrayal.

CHAPTER SEVEN

The Torso

Officers picked their way along the banks of the River Boyne, in fields at the back of Gerard 'Ged' McKenna's Rathmullan Park home and in sports grounds in Drogheda, all of which had been areas identified as possible dumping grounds for Keane Mulready-Woods' missing torso. It was a gruesome task and a constant reminder of the horrors that had been visited on the 17-year-old on the night of his death. The information provided to gardaí by secret informers had proved to be rock-solid. Not only had they identified the crime scene very early on in the investigation, they had also been able to piece together a motive, albeit one that made sense only in the twisted mind of the man responsible for the murder, Robbie Lawlor. It was the affront to the criminal carried out when the group of young men, mostly aligned to Mr Big, had confronted him on a street and stolen his gym bag that had led him to snatch the teenager and dismember his body. In Lawlor's mind, Mulready-Woods had been playing both sides and he'd convinced himself he had something to do with his brother-in-law's murder. Those who knew him would later admit that Lawlor's mental health had taken a dive in the last few years of his life, and around the time he targeted Fiona Mitchell in a rage over his ex-girlfriend's relationship with her son, he was displaying bizarre facial twitches. Lawlor's cocaine and steroid use could certainly go some of the way to explaining his increasing rift with reality, but he'd been hot-headed and impulsive all his life. However, despite his ability to think and act quickly, he actually had a clear plan when he organised luring Keane Mulready-Woods to Rathmullan Park. The team investigating the murder had been told that Lawlor's intention was to dump the teenager's head and torso at rival Cornelius Price's compound in Gormanston and his legs near the neighbourhoods associated with Mr Big and his army of youngsters who'd photographed themselves wearing his flip-flops.

It appeared that things hadn't quite gone to plan. The chaotic setting on fire of the car in Dublin containing the head, feet and hands of the teenager was proof to officers that panic had finally set in and those delivering the body parts had dumped them and run. The torso, officers now believed, could have been flung into waste ground around the compound or been delivered at some point. To Lawlor, dumping the body parts might have been a game, but officers were painfully aware that the situation was not only a hugely emotional issue for the family but also a technical one for the murder team – without the torso they had no cause of death. In the weeks since his murder, Gardaí had made huge headway with the inquiry into Keane Mulready-Woods' murder and had identified the four men they believed had a role to play in his gruesome death.

The importance of the immediate intelligence that had led them to the home of Gerard 'Ged' McKenna in Rathmullan Park couldn't be overstated as it was there that forensics had found the scene of the crime freshly painted in a crude bid to cover up what had happened. A search warrant for the house had been issued on foot of confidential information and gardaí had entered it around 4.50pm on 14 January, just two days after they believed Keane had been killed there. They found McKenna at home watching television but noticed a strong smell of paint. Inquiries had since found that he had painted over bloodstains and other evidence. Despite his efforts, splashes and splatters were clearly visible on the ceilings and upper walls and forensics later recovered Keane's blood in a number of different parts of the house. Officers had also discovered blood and DNA along with remnants of his clothing and the ballistic vest he'd been wearing when he disappeared in a fire that had been lit at the back of the house.

McKenna, a father of eight, had lived in the council bungalow at Rathmullan Park for years. He was a drinker and drug user who'd known the Mulready-Woods families from Drogheda, where he'd grown up, but he was also associated with low-level members of the anti-Maguire group and was known as someone who would do jobs for drinking money. When gardaí arrived to search his home, he claimed that he knew nothing, but they found an L-shaped couch that he'd dragged outside, and phone records showed that McKenna had received a call from Paul Crosby before the murder and had left his house immediately afterwards. Officers had found a box of penknives in a green area near the property; and an axe, socks and bone fragments had been found in a car searched as part of the inquiry. While teams of officers combed the house and took away boxes of evidence, others were concentrating on the mobile phone traffic between the suspects and the CCTV images that showed them moving around in the hours before and after the killing.

Records showed that Crosby phoned Keane Mulready-Woods at 5.57pm on 12 January and the teenager left his home immediately afterwards in a taxi. At the Centra shop in Ballsgrove he met with Crosby, who paid the fare, and the two got into a Volkswagen car belonging to Gerard Cruise. Cruise was considered a lackey who'd been working on and off for Crosby as a driver. His last conviction, for possession of drugs, was from 2010; and prior to that he hadn't been in trouble since the 1990s when he got a few convictions for public order offences and a burglary. Then in his late 40s, he had four children and several grandchildren, and worked on and off as a manual labourer. Inquiries had found that Cruise had been involved in the purchase of a car before the murder and false number plates in the aftermath; these were placed on the vehicle used to drive the holdall to Coolock. CCTV showed Cruise, Crosby and Lawlor at the back of the McKenna home at 6.48pm that night with Keane Mulready-Woods, a blurry image which would mark the last time the teenager was photographed alive. Mobile phone records also showed that Crosby and Lawlor were in touch on the afternoon of the murder, and they were by far the most important suspects in the case. They were a match made in hell.

Crosby, who'd goaded Owen Maguire in that notorious phone call, equalled Lawlor's violence and impulsiveness. Aged just 25, he was known as being highly dangerous and unpredictable and had 40 convictions for drugs, theft, criminal damage and even arson. The previous February he had been acquitted of attempted murder, the second time he'd stood trial for the stabbing of a man who'd been lucky to escape with his life. Both trials heard that in 2016 Gerard Boyle had been stabbed 28 times before being shoved into the boot of a car which was then pushed into a canal. Despite suffering a punctured lung he had managed to escape and swim to safety. Months after Crosby's acquittal the Emergency Response Unit had been watching Crosby when he was seen trying to jump start a stolen car at an industrial estate in Drogheda. Once it was started, he and a group with him had driven it to a field, where it was set on fire. Officers had seen this as an opportunity to get him into prison while the feud in Drogheda was reaching its peak; however, while Crosby had been charged with arson, he'd got bail.

Lawlor, officers believed, had been the director of operations on the night of the murder and had personally flung the sports bag containing the teenager's legs onto a pavement at Moatview. They also believed that he personally planned to deliver the head and torso to Cornelius Price to remind him that he should never have crossed him in prison. Delving into the twisted mind of Lawlor, officers could see the complexities of the plan, which ticked many boxes for him and served as revenge for the murder of Richie Carberry. However, it hadn't all gone exactly to plan.

Without the torso, investigators were concerned that they could have difficulty getting a murder conviction for any of the killers; they knew that at the very least they would be facing huge difficulties should they get them to a court of law. Forensic evidence discovered at the house in Rathmullan Park, in the field behind it and from the cars used in the sickening plot left no doubt but that Keane had been stabbed to death before he was dismembered, but without the pathology to prove it the case would have to be based on circumstantial evidence.

The cause of death is vital in almost all criminal cases. The burden of proof for murder lies entirely with the State and evidence has to be accepted beyond reasonable doubt. Without the torso, there were no certainties and the man at the very top of the investigation team was painfully aware that sometimes, no matter what resources there were, body parts might never be found. In one of his most high-profile previous cases, Mangan had done everything in his power to complete the remains of a dismembered victim, Farah Swaleh Noor, whose body parts had been found floating in the Royal Canal near Croke Park, north Dublin, in March 2005. A Kenyan national, he had been beaten and his body dismembered at a nearby house in Ballybough by the Mulhall sisters, Charlotte and Linda. While the cause of death was stabbing, and not in dispute during the case, gardaí had never recovered his head or private parts, which had been dumped in a different part of the city. Mangan had even brought Linda Mulhall back to the Tallaght park where she said she had first buried the head, only to later dig it up before re-interring it. Mulhall had told Mangan that she had carried the head in a backpack on a bus and later through a shopping centre as she made her way to the park where she disposed of it.

In the more recent case of Graham Dwyer, charged with the murder of Elaine O'Hara, the absence of a cause of death had been a key problem point for the prosecution. Dwyer had pleaded not guilty to the murder of childcare worker Elaine at Killakee Mountain on 22 August 2012. Her partial remains were discovered there in September 2013 but they were so badly decomposed no cause of death could be determined. Under cross-examination, Deputy State Pathologist Dr Michael Curtis had told the trial that only 60–65 per cent of Ms O'Hara's bones had been recovered on the Dublin mountain and that neither foul play nor self-harm could be ruled out. Text messages between two phones named Slave and Master that were discovered dumped in a reservoir in Roundwood, and which the prosecution said belonged to Elaine O'Hara and Dwyer, formed the backbone of the State's evidence against Dwyer. In them he told her he was sexually aroused by pain and blood and said his ultimate fantasy was to stab a woman to death. He directed her to the shoreline at Shankill on the day she disappeared and had earlier warned her he was planning 'big punishment' and she would be 'knifed in the guts, and well bound and gagged, deep in a forest'.

'You will do what you are told during play and follow instruction,' he texted, adding, 'I have found a remote place, no one will find us.' The court had also seen deeply disturbing videos Dwyer had made of BDSM sex sessions he had had with Elaine and other women during which Ms O'Hara was heard whimpering and asking him to stop. Graphic pornography he had written to another would-be victim was also read to the court in which he described climaxing while stabbing a woman to death and then repeatedly raping her dead body. Exactly how Elaine died was never established, but overwhelming circumstantial evidence saw Dwyer jailed for life for murder.

As politicians continued to condemn the killing of Keane Mulready-Woods and the wheels of justice moved slowly against the suspects, the issue of cocaine settled firmly into the national agenda. Within days of the murder, former senior Garda Michael O'Sullivan, who was by then heading up the Marine Analysis and Operations Centre (MAOC) in Lisbon, announced that the agency responsible for co-ordinating activities in European Union countries had seized a record-breaking €2.1 billion worth of cocaine on the high seas in 2019. As war raged in Drogheda, MAOC had swooped on 17 different vessels carrying a combined total of just under 25 tonnes of the drug towards Europe. The contraband had included 9.5 tonnes of high-purity cocaine seized off the small island of Cape Verde and three tonnes found in a semi-submersible vessel near Galicia in Spain, the first time such a boat had been used for a transatlantic crossing. 'There is more cocaine being produced and there are more vessels coming in. The European cocaine market grew to €9.1 billion last year, a 60 per cent increase in three years. And that's just for cocaine. This is driving gangland violence such as the murder and dismemberment of seventeen-year-old Keane Mulready-Woods,' O'Sullivan said.

Mangan echoed his sentiments:

> He is a child of a lost generation. It is terribly sad. One of our first victims of 2020 is a child lost to drug dealers. Cocaine is

a cultural and social problem. Not all users are going to get in trouble with the guards. The majority of users are able to go to a housing estate, buy cocaine and then snort it in their social venues, they are professionals, sports people who are never going to come into contact with the guards. They are the people that are propping up the drug dealers and the likes of the people who killed Keane. They are the people that have contributed in a huge way to this social problem. And they think it's cool. You are contributing to the machine that's killing people . . . I think we have to attach responsibility to the people involved in consuming cocaine. Some will ignore it but there will be a percentage of people who will say I am that person who bought that drug off Mr X who may have been involved in the death of Keane.

Violent crime was centre stage in the general election campaign, with Fianna Fáil leader Micheál Martin accusing the government of 'losing control'. He said 'drug terrorism' was as much a threat to society as the IRA had been in the past. 'People deserve much better from their government. It is four years since the murder at the Regency Hotel and there have been almost thirty gang-related murders since. We have reached a tipping point and these gangs have to be crushed.' Taoiseach Leo Varadkar defended his party record on tackling crime and insisted Ireland was safe: 'Ireland is a country that is safe. Ireland is a country that thankfully relative to other countries has a relatively low crime rate and a relatively low murder rate. That doesn't detract in any way from the seriousness of the crimes that we have witnessed.' As calls for more gardaí, tougher legislation and a crackdown on cocaine came fast and furious, gardaí realised that the feud would likely play itself out before the justice system could catch up.

Many key players were feeling the heat, including the two brothers who'd challenged the power of Maguire and Price in the first place. They had gone to ground and had failed to sign in at a Garda station. Facing trial for false imprisonment in relation to the incident in Drogheda in November 2018, when gardaí had rescued a young man from their captivity, they'd gone on the run in fear of their lives and left their lawyers at home to explain where they were. It soon emerged they had skipped the country and were lying low in Spain. After a brief stint at home, Cornelius Price had returned to the UK, where he bedded down with relatives in the Rochdale area and where he enjoyed far less attention from police. With armed gardaí on the streets 24 hours a day, Drogheda was safer than it had been in years, with almost half of all the feuding gang members keeping a low profile in the belief that they'd be arrested or shot.

Meetings between the senior Garda units like the CAB and the Drugs and Organised Crime Bureau concentrated on the gangs of Drogheda as the State placed its full force behind ending the bloodshed for good. Communities began to feel empowered for the first time in years and towards the end of January thousands of people turned out for a rally against violence in the town, a gathering organised by the mayor, Paul Bell, who announced that the only business going forward was to take the town back from the criminals. 'No siege and no force can defeat the spirit of what makes Drogheda citizens so special and people will not fail in ridding the communities of those who are convinced they are untouchable and free to do as they please,' he said. Despite this dogged spirit, investigators were still anxious to recover the torso and in a bid to talk to anyone who had information on its whereabouts Superintendent Andy Watters went on RTÉ's *Crimecall* to make a direct appeal to the conscience of those linked to the crime. He asked for the information on behalf of the family and also urged people not to share the unverified crime scene image. While criminals from both sides saw the writing on the wall, Robbie Lawlor was undeterred. In a show of brazen defiance he visited Darndale and Kilbarrack, calling to the homes of a number of associates before settling in for a pint in a local pub, news that quickly spread.

A month after he had been reported missing, a white coffin bearing an image of a scrambler motorbike held the partial remains of Keane Mulready-Woods during his funeral service at the Church of the Holy Family in Ballsgrove in Drogheda. While his family had insisted they wouldn't bury him until his torso was found, they had accepted the stark reality that they might never get all his body parts back. For four weeks his estranged parents Elizabeth and Barry, sister Courtney and brothers Darren, Ryan and Jack had been bombarded by the gruesome headlines and the social media postings, but finally it seemed time to lay him to rest. At the service, the floral tributes, including those depicting the Gucci label that Keane had loved to wear, rested on his coffin. Fr Phil Gaffney tried to make sense of what had happened, delivering a carefully crafted homily to the packed church.

> Our first reaction today is one of great sympathy for Keane's parents and family for the great crime committed against a

brother and a son, for the great wrong that was done to them. Along with that there has to be great anger and even sadness, great fear and pain perhaps, at the thought that we live in a society where certain people took it upon themselves to play god with regard to the life of Keane Mulready-Woods. They took it upon themselves to be judge, jury and executioner. What arrogance! What appalling wickedness and evil. To say that the death of Keane has shocked and appalled the town of Drogheda would be a total understatement. This young man, at the time not eighteen years of age, has been lost in the most gruesome way to his family. We know that Keane's tragic death has devastated you. We all want to reach out to you with love and reassurance. We all want to gather around you and to uphold you. We want to mourn with you. We want to pray with you for Keane.

Directly addressing the countless young men in the congregation, each dressed in the designer clothes that Keane had lived and died in, the priest urged them to turn their back on drugs and the life they afforded them.

> Keane had his troubles and was young and naive enough to fall in with the wrong people, not knowing or anticipating the dire consequences. I hope that his death will be a warning to other young teenagers who are being groomed by the ruthless criminals on the promise of money and gifts which will inevitably end in tragedy. Keane's association with them sadly led to the inhuman, unthinkable way his young life was to end . . . And this is what confuses us now. Keane's death seems so utterly inappropriate. It violates our sense of order. In our

view of life, death and childhood are poles apart, and seventeen years simply does not seem the right time to die – it does not seem to add up . . . I want to say a special word of condolence to Keane's young friends. Please learn from his mistakes, getting involved with dangerous criminals, thinking some of them were his friends and yet they would sacrifice him in such a brutal manner.

Gardaí who attended the service hoped too that it would deter other young children from joining gangs, but they knew that teenagers were very much part and parcel of the warring groups in Drogheda and always had been. Half the members of both the Price–Maguire gang and their rivals, each more than forty strong, were under the age of 25 and at least one in every five was a teenager.

As the cortège made its way to Calvary Cemetery in the town where a freshly dug grave awaited, many ignored the pleas of the priest and plotted their next move. Meanwhile Robbie Lawlor was on the move, travelling to and from Belfast, where he was working as a debt collector and even planning a holiday in Spain. Days after the funeral, on 20 February, Ged McKenna and Gerard Cruise were arrested in early morning swoops and taken to separate Garda stations under Section 50 of the Criminal Justice Act. The news made huge headlines. Eight days later McKenna was charged with impeding the apprehension of a prosecution of another person in relation to the murder. A large crowd gathered outside Drogheda District Court, where he tried to hide his face with a jacket. He was remanded in custody while files on the others were being prepared for the Director of Public Prosecutions.

But as the net began to tighten on the gangs of Drogheda and gardaí started to regain their control over the town, another force was looming which would prove to be a foe far more difficult to contain. Just weeks after the brutal murder of Keane Mulready-Woods, the World Health Organization declared a 'public health emergency of international concern'. It was in late February, when 'Ged' McKenna was being led off to jail, when Ireland's very first case of Covid-19 was confirmed by the Department of Health; a teenage boy, just back from northern Italy, was being treated in a Dublin hospital. By 11 March it was officially declared that the coronavirus outbreak was a pandemic, the first to hit the world since the flu pandemic of 1918. On that same day it was confirmed that the first Irish person had died from the virus, an elderly woman with an underlying health condition in County Kildare. The next day Taoiseach Leo Varadkar ordered the shutdown of schools, colleges and public places, while outdoor gatherings of over 500 and indoor gatherings of over 100 people were banned. At the time, the global death toll stood at more than 4,600.

Just two days before St Patrick's Day the pubs were ordered to shut their doors and on 17 March, Varadkar made his first public address on Covid-19.

> Today's children will tell their own grandchildren about the national holiday in 2020 that had no parades or parties . . . but instead saw everyone staying at home to protect each other. In years to come . . . let them say of us . . . when things were at their worst . . . we were at our best . . . Not all superheroes wear capes . . . some wear scrubs and gowns . . . This is the calm before the storm.

Ten days later, as cases continued to skyrocket, Ireland was put on an initial two-week lockdown, and all non-essential journeys were banned. The public were only permitted to leave their houses to go to the shops to buy food or medical supplies, or if they needed to provide vital family care for the elderly and vulnerable. They could also leave home for brief periods of physical exercise, as long as they stayed within a 2km radius of their home. While ordinary citizens sat at home, wondering where it was all going to end and if the virus was coming for them, the eyes of the law were on the criminal underworld, a community reluctant to ever follow any laws. Would a pandemic be enough to curb them too?

On 2 April 2020 a headline in the *Irish Independent* was like music to the ears of the town dogged by the drug feud: 'Drug seizures and lockdown bring lull to deadly gang feud.' The article detailed how a combination of Garda seizures and restrictions on movement as a result of the coronavirus had led to a virtual lull in the tit-for-tat attacks in the Drogheda feud. Just two days later that myth would be shattered by a hail of bullets in the most unlikely of places for Robbie Lawlor to fall.

CHAPTER EIGHT

The Murder of a Killer

Ardoyne in north Belfast is often described as a rabbit warren, with rows upon rows of identical red-brick terraced houses lying in the shadow of the Divis Mountain and bordered to the west by the largely Protestant Crumlin Road. With giant murals commemorating the 1916 Easter Rising and those killed during the Troubles, visitors can have no illusion as to where allegiances lie. Working-class and decidedly Catholic, this tiny corner of Belfast, with a population of just over a thousand, has had more than its fair share of headline-making events, from the mass riots during marching season to parents and their bewildered children being led by Fr Aidan Troy to the Holy Cross school through crowds of baying loyalists in the early 2000s. But April 2020 brought an event that would, in many ways, prove that the underbelly of society in Belfast had changed. Now it was far more about drugs than the politics of the past.

The early weeks of the pandemic, when Covid lockdowns became part of ordinary life, were particularly warm and sunny, and residents of Ardoyne had decamped to their small front gardens. While fears were growing that a surge of coronavirus cases would cripple the health services and create a worldwide recession, one bit of good news for the people of Ardoyne was that the pandemic meant the notorious Twelfth of July parades had been cancelled. The Orange Order had announced that they had made the decision in the interests of public safety; this was the first time since the Second World War that its members had agreed to lay down their drums. On Etna Drive, the morning of Saturday 4 April felt like a summer's day and adults sat on deckchairs while children played nearby. Sometime before midday a blue Volvo car drove down the road and pulled up outside number 61, a house that had been somewhat unlived in since its owner had passed away, leaving it to a number of family members including a grandson, Adrian 'Aidy' Holland, who stayed there sporadically. Holland was well known to PSNI officers as someone who associated with a number of criminals, but he had no reputation for violence and was largely seen as a wheeler dealer who could source a car and manage a few logistics. A man got out of the Volvo and started walking towards the door but then there was a flash and the unmistakable noise of gunshots shattered the midday air. One, two, three, four the bullets came and in an instant the Volvo had sped off and a body lay in the front garden of the house. In the distance those who witnessed the broad daylight murder could hear another car speeding from the back of the house and screeching away. Ten minutes later, as police attended the scene of the murder, another unit was called to nearby Kingston Court where the burnt-out shell of a silver VW Scirocco was discovered.

While Ardoyne had seen its fair share of sectarian violence it was not the natural scene for a gangland shooting and within an hour rumours about the identity of the murdered man had reached fever pitch. Some initially believed that it was Holland who had been killed, but witnesses said they had seen him alive and well nearby. By the time the name Robbie Lawlor was being whispered, people were openly questioning what a 'Dublin' drug dealer was doing in the republican enclave in the first place. Without any evidence, many were suggesting that he'd been eradicated for simply thinking he could flex his muscles in Belfast. The truth was far more complex than that and would ultimately form part of a picture of a new underworld, where loyalty was no longer to unionism or republicanism but only to the business of money.

Inside the gates of number 61, forensic officers quickly began their task of combing the scene for clues to the killing. A tent was erected over Lawlor's body so that any fragments of evidence could be carefully gathered, and inside the house the painstaking process of harvesting any DNA available began. What was clear to those investigating the scene was that Lawlor had no clue he was under threat when he got out of the car and walked towards the door of the house at Etna Drive. He was wearing no ballistics vest or bullet-resistant clothing and he was dressed casually. His killer, it appeared, had run at him from the house, then turned to make his getaway through the back door and out onto the laneway that ran behind the house. While it would have to be confirmed by whatever CCTV could be gathered in the weeks ahead, officers were also pretty certain that the burnt-out Scirocco was a getaway vehicle and that the gunman would have likely been picked up near Kingston Court by a second car.

It didn't take long for news of the demise of one of gangland's most wanted men to filter across the border and to the Gardaí, who awaited official confirmation that the body in the garden in Ardoyne was Lawlor's. But when members of the Lawlor family started to make panicked calls they realised that there was no mistaking who was dead. By Saturday afternoon, while his body still lay outside the house in Etna Drive, the scale of the story meant that crime correspondents were dispatched across the border into the North, despite the travel restrictions. In Belfast, sources told mixed tales around the reason for Lawlor's death. Many suggested that he had tried to muscle in on the drug scene and had been taken out by dissident republicans intent on keeping their areas clean of dealers. Others suggested that he had crossed the line with rivals with his fast tongue and southern confidence. Suspicions surrounded Lawlor's arrival at Etna Drive. Had he been there to carry out a hit himself, only for the tide to turn on him? Was he collecting a car or trying to force a drug debt from someone unable to pay it? Given Lawlor's reputation and his past employment as both a killer and an enforcer, along with his increasingly chaotic existence since the murder of Keane Mulready-Woods, one thing that everyone could agree on was that anything was possible. Rarely had a murder victim amassed so many enemies or blazed a trail the likes of Robbie Lawlor, but what remained a mystery was why Belfast? And why an area like Ardoyne, where once drug dealers from the Republic would literally not have been caught dead?

Very quickly the PSNI moved to piece together information around the movements of cars they suspected to have been used in the murder. The Scirocco was the best clue they had to go on from the outset, and Detective Superintendent Jason Murphy, who was leading the investigation, felt it was vital to appeal for information while the events of the day were still fresh in the mind of the public.

> I am astounded by the recklessness of the killer or killers. Not only did they carry out this callous murder, leaving a family experiencing their worst nightmare, but they did not care that children and other members of this north Belfast community were placed at risk. Murder is a heinous crime and killing someone during this global coronavirus pandemic is sickening when people are trying to adjust to living a new way and trying to cope with the pressures this brings. A light-coloured car, registration YLZ 7052, was found burnt out in Kingston Court and I am currently seeking to establish what relevance this car has to my investigation. I know the community is in shock at the moment but I would appeal to anyone who has information about this appalling murder to bring that information forward to the police so that we can remove this dangerous gunman and his associates from our streets.

While the PSNI were liaising with the Gardaí and both police forces were swapping intelligence and using their well-established investigation techniques to gather evidence, something far more futuristic was happening in the background of the Lawlor murder which would help to uncover one of the most sinister and cunning double-crosses the underworld has ever seen.

Since 2017 the French Gendarmerie had been investigating phones that used the secured communication tool EncroChat after repeatedly finding the handsets during operations against organised crime groups. The phones came with a guarantee to users of absolute anonymity and total discretion, with add-ons like the automatic deletion of messages should the phones be seized or lost. EncroChat was not the first encrypted system to become popular among criminal groupings, but it was seen as the most secure. Word of mouth had led to the company gaining more than 60,000 customers all over Europe. At some point police in France discovered that the company was operating from servers at Roubaix near Lille and they managed to place a technical device there – under French law it is illegal to supply cryptographic services without notifying the government. By early 2020 EncroChat was one of the most widely used encrypted phone services among the criminal underworld and France was on the brink of being able to hack it. Authorities reached out to the Netherlands, seen as European leaders in crypto-hacking, and to Eurojust (the EU's Agency for Criminal Justice Cooperation), in order to create a data pathway for the thousands of messages they hoped they would soon be able to see. The plan was to funnel all messages to a central control and then pass them on to member countries depending on what information was deemed relevant to them or what could be listened to in live time. The hack had gone live on 1 April, just days before Lawlor was shot, and the flow of information to intelligence wings of police in countries including the UK and Ireland had begun. And while it is safe to assume that the planning of the Lawlor hit had not been picked up on EncroChat, some of the strange events that happened in its aftermath occurred as a direct result of the ability of police to eavesdrop on phones.

Hours after he was shot dead, the PSNI arrested three men who they described as being with Lawlor in the run-up to his murder and driving the Volvo car which he'd been in minutes before he was killed. Ger Dundon, Levi Killeen and Quincy Bramble were no strangers to gardaí south of the border, but they were less well known to the PSNI. Ger Dundon, in his thirties, was one of the notorious Dundon brothers from Limerick who'd blazed a trail of terror over a decade in gang wars that had resulted in almost twenty murders. Unlike his brothers Wayne, John and Dessie, who were all serving life sentences for murder, Ger had been in and out of the prison system on lesser charges. Living between London and Limerick, he had a hefty rap sheet involving more than a hundred convictions around weapons, intimidation, violence and robbery. His nephew Levi Killeen was just 17 years old, the son of John, who was serving time for the murder of innocent rugby player Shane Geoghegan. Levi had lived with his mother Ciara Killeen since his father's imprisonment and together they'd fortified their home on Limerick's Hyde Road, where the Dundons had once ruled with an iron fist. His uncle Nathan Killeen was also serving a life sentence along with Wayne for the 2009 murder of the innocent man Roy Collins. Levi's grandmother Susan, who was also originally from Hyde Road, had died at the age of 54 when she was found drowned with toxic levels of alcohol in her blood. She'd been plucked from the canal at Lock Quay in Limerick. At the coroner's court her daughter Ciara had said her mother was living with her and 'not in a great place mentally' at the time of her death. It was around the same time that Ger Dundon's former partner April Collins agreed to give evidence at the Special Criminal Court against his brother John. She'd testified that John had been shouting at killer Barry Doyle after the murder of Shane Geoghegan that he'd 'shot the wrong man'. Despite his youth, Levi commanded respect among his elders and was a keen boxer, just like his uncles Wayne and Ger. Bramble was an associate of Dundon and regularly travelled with him between Limerick and the UK.

It was easy to see how the Dundons could have been involved in setting up Robbie Lawlor. After all, the mob had staged the most spectacular double-cross in gangland history when they had set up their own rival Kieran Keane back in 2003 when a kidnap was staged and he was lured to a meeting and to his death. However, officers discovered that the car that Ger Dundon had been driving had been hit by bullets too and in custody he had immediately said he'd screeched out of Ardoyne, leaving Lawlor dead on Etna Drive, and claimed he was in fear for his life. In custody, Ger Dundon took control of the narrative, telling officers that he was a friend of Lawlor and insinuating he was prepared to bear witness against anyone they intended to charge. He'd phoned the Lawlor family, he said, when he realised his pal had been killed, and he'd been the one to break the news to them.

When officers from the PSNI sought clarification of the relationship between Dundon and Lawlor from their colleagues south of the border they were told that the pair had been close associates since they met in prison and when Lawlor hired Ger Dundon to act as a bodyguard for him after he'd been attacked and slashed on the orders of Cornelius Price. At the time Dundon was serving a sentence handed down by the Special Criminal Court for helping to hide a sawn-off automatic pump-action shotgun in the outside toilet of a house while Lawlor was awaiting trial for threats to kill Rachel Kirwan and Fiona Mitchell. The duo had both been released from prison around the same time and Ger Dundon had been operating as a driver and a protector for Lawlor ever since, intelligence stated.

Later that evening members of the PSNI arrested Warren Crossan at his Belfast home. The 28-year-old was the son of well-known dissident republican Tommy Crossan, who'd been shot dead on the Springfield Road in Belfast in 2014. After the murder Warren had built himself up into a major drug dealer and had been sourcing cocaine in Dublin and smuggling it across the border in specially designed vehicles. He'd also been importing prescription drugs, mainly Xanax, from England to Northern Ireland, where there was a huge market among a population traumatised by years of the Troubles. Crossan was ambitious and ruthless. Holland was among his many associates, but he also knew Ger Dundon and had met with him shortly after the murder.

While detectives worked on their suspects, videos began to spread on social media as enemies of Robbie Lawlor celebrated his death. One clip showed a dozens-strong group of young men partying and drinking in the front garden of a house in Dublin as music blared on a speaker. In another video Cornelius Price raised a glass of Captain Morgan rum and spoke directly into the camera. 'Here's to Robbie Lawlor, rest in peace – he's not even worth saying rest in peace ... Fair play to ye, Lee.' Another showed a woman closely associated with David Lynch singing and dancing in a kitchen among a group of others. Associates of Keane Mulready-Woods also took to social media to express their delight.

By the following day, headlines screamed that Lawlor had been in Belfast to collect a drug debt or even to murder someone himself when things had backfired. Politicians lined up to give their opinion on the murder and to focus on the fact that organised crime gangs had failed to respect the Covid 19 lockdowns. Ruairí Ó Murchú, a Sinn Féin TD for County Louth, reassured the public that gardaí would not let up their efforts against organised criminal and drug gangs, despite their increased policing responsibilities due to the Covid-19 crisis.

> Anecdotally, cocaine supply in the county has declined massively since the coronavirus outbreak, but drug dealers continue to supply heroin and other drugs. With the decline of the recreational cocaine market, it means, however, that drug gangs are turning the screw even harder on those whom they claim owe them money, leading to further fear and terror in local families because of drug debt intimidation. However, I understand that gardaí are continuing to strike against organised and drug criminals and have carried out a number of successful operations in the division over the last

couple of weeks, despite the fact that they have additional duties because of the Covid-19 crisis. I want to commend them for that.

Back in the North, the murder had sent shockwaves across the province and the PSNI's Chief Constable Simon Byrne visited Ardoyne. Northern Secretary Brandon Lewis released a statement calling the murder an abhorrent and brutal crime for which there was no excuse. 'This cowardly act is particularly thoughtless at a time when our frontline emergency services are already working incredibly hard to keep us all safe while dealing with the impact of the Covid-19 pandemic,' he said. Politicians from all sides sent out similar messages of disgust and outrage, including North Belfast SDLP councillor Paul McCusker, who said people in Ardoyne were in total shock. 'This brutal crime has caused immense shock in Ardoyne today,' he said. 'A man was shot in a garden in this community in broad daylight. It's hard to describe how traumatic this has been for people who were going about their business.' Detective Superintendent Murphy soon made use of the publicity surrounding the murder in a bid to get information for his inquiry.

> I believe a single gunman was involved in the killing, firing multiple shots at the victim and striking him a number of times. The murder weapon has not yet been recovered. I do not believe that Robbie Lawlor was in the Ardoyne yesterday by accident. I believe he had some reason to be there and key lines of enquiry for me at this stage are to establish why he was there and what his connection to the address is.

In the early hours of Sunday morning, less than 24 hours after being arrested, Levi Killeen was released unconditionally. Ger Dundon and Quincy Bramble remained in custody, but by Monday morning just Warren Crossan was left. Over the weekend relatives of Lawlor had travelled north to identify his body, while a former associate of Richie Carberry was told that his life was under threat. The brothers who led the anti-Maguire faction had fled for Spain and intelligence suggested that Price's mob had circulated an image showing three Smirnoff bottles symbolising three rivals shot: Lawlor, Carberry and Brannigan. Two bottles covered in brown cloth represented the on-the-run Drogheda brothers with the subliminal message that their contents would only be drunk in celebration when they were killed.

At the same time as Ger Dundon and Quincy Bramble were released from custody in the North an undercover operation was playing out in the South. Officers were aware that the Maguire organisation had arranged the transfer of a large sum of cash to the Dundon mob through two female associates who were preparing to meet for the pick-up. The intelligence was so good it would be hard to dismiss the probability that it came from the EncroChat hack. As undercover officers watched the Midway Food Court in Portlaoise, they saw Dessie Dundon's long-term girlfriend Ciara Lynch and her friend Kathleen O'Reilly pull in. It was about 1pm and Lynch was driving a Mercedes A-Class with an altered registration plate. O'Reilly, who lived at a Limerick halting site, was the front seat passenger.

Lynch had lived in the bosom of the Dundon mob for years despite the fact that she had only met her 'partner' in prison at the age of 12 when she went to visit someone else. Dundon had caught her eye and their union had been sealed, despite the fact that he hadn't enjoyed a single day of freedom since. Lynch moved in with the Dundons in Dessie's home on the Hyde Road, a barricaded property next door to Ciara Killeen, to wait for his eventual release from prison for the murder of Kieran Keane. Lynch had previously proved herself deeply loyal to Dundon. She had three previous convictions and had received a suspended sentence for violent disorder in 2011. This offence had arisen in 2010 when, after a row at Limerick Prison, she turned up at Alice Collins's house with three other women and attacked her car with a sledge hammer. Collins was the mother of April, the former partner of Ger Dundon, who'd agreed to give evidence on behalf of the State. Lynch was acquitted a year later of intimidating Alice and April Collins before they were to testify against John and Wayne Dundon.

As gardaí watched the Midway Food Court they saw a man approach the Mercedes carrying a Mr Price shopping bag and waited until he handed it through the front passenger window of the car. Lynch started to drive away but was stopped by officers on the M7 as she drove in the direction of Limerick. In the bag they found €50,000 in used €50 notes. Later, under cross-examination in court, a detective accepted that O'Reilly was not a member of a criminal gang in Limerick or anywhere else, and that she had no role in organising the handover of money.

Despite the activities south of the border, officers investigating the murder concentrated on the car that had been burnt after Robbie Lawlor was shot. The PSNI released details that the getaway car had been parked in Estoril Park in Ardoyne at 10am on the Friday, the day before the murder, but that it had been stolen in the Republic on 30 January. They also stated that they wanted to speak to a hooded man. Detective Chief Inspector Peter Montgomery said: 'I have received reports of a person, wearing a black jacket with the hood up, carrying a holdall while walking along Jamaica Way towards Oldpark Road.' It was there that detectives had identified a black Audi A3 parked up in the early morning before the hit on Lawlor and that had disappeared ten minutes after the death of the hitman.

CHAPTER NINE

A Romance and a Double-Cross

Despite the demise of Robbie Lawlor and the celebrations on social media that followed his death, gardaí were not convinced that they had seen the end of the murder and mayhem that had turned the town of Drogheda into a gangland wild west. As PSNI officers in the North pieced together the vital 24 hours before the murder and the movement of particular cars around Belfast, their colleagues in Drogheda were dealing with a highly unusual fall-out from the hit. Days after the murder, and as Lawlor's family began preparations for his funeral, a blonde professional met with officers and handed them a note she had received at her home address. It contained, she said, accurate information around her movements in the weeks before Lawlor's murder and chilling accounts of attempts to assassinate him while he was in her company. For officers, the note was curious in many ways. Aside from its sinister message, it was extremely well written and articulate and while it was suspected that it had come straight from those who'd planned and directed the Lawlor hit, it suggested far more literacy skills than Cornelius Price or Owen Maguire were known to have command of.

The woman had been an enigma to many who knew her. A middle-class, educated, successful businesswoman who worked on the legal side of criminality in a role that had brought her into close proximity with many undesirable characters, she was the last woman many would expect to enter into a relationship with a dangerous and volatile figure like Robbie Lawlor. Her arrival at Drogheda Garda Station with the note detailing liaisons with Lawlor was not a total shock to detectives. Officers had first noticed a strange closeness between her and Lawlor when he once placed flowers on the four doors of her car near a courtroom. The strange act, witnessed by officers who were watching him from a distance, had caused concern – it was initially assumed that Lawlor was trying to threaten or intimidate her or that he was making unwanted romantic gestures to her. It was decided that gardaí would approach the woman and let her know what had happened and that if she had any concerns in either regard the full force of the law would be behind her; nobody would stand back and let a dangerous criminal like Lawlor frighten her. The reaction of the woman, who smiled and blushed like a giddy schoolgirl, told officers that something far more bizarre was going on and it soon became apparent that the pair were in a relationship, despite his reputation and the differences in their backgrounds. To make matters more inappropriate, officers were aware that the woman had business dealings with Owen Maguire and other rivals of Lawlor who, they believed, did not know of the clandestine relationship. However, the note told them a different story and they realised that the woman's life was in immediate danger.

The strange relationship between the woman and Lawlor had in the past concerned Chief Superintendent Christy Mangan to such an extent that he had written to Garda Commissioner Drew Harris to inform him about it and to raise his concerns about the type of business she was conducting throughout the region. Despite his intervention it would later emerge that the woman had applied for an administrative role in CAB and had made it to the last two candidates. Those interviewing her were unaware of her closeness to Lawlor, which could have left her open to blackmail or extortion.

The detailed information in the note included a date when, the writer claimed, gunmen had been watching the woman's house late one night, believing Lawlor to be inside. It gave the exact location of the property and a detailed description, including a timestamp when, it was alleged, a security light had come on and forced the gunman to retreat from the property. It gave details of other addresses where, the writer claimed, plots to kill had come unstuck for other reasons. The letter warned the woman not to attend the funeral and gave accurate accounts of her own regular movements, including gym classes and visits to family. The woman was already way out of her depth when it came to Robbie Lawlor's life and death. The PSNI wanted to talk to her about her own movements around the time of his murder. They had been told that she had been planning to bring Lawlor's children to Belfast to see him on the day of his murder and that she had driven up to collect some of his personal effects after he was gunned down and despite an investigation being under way. The information had come from other criminals caught up in the shooting, but the PSNI hoped that she would present herself for questioning about the claims and clear up the allegations. Despite the detail in the note and the suggestions that dangerous lieutenants of Price, Maguire and even Mr Big had had her under surveillance for weeks before the murder, the woman still wanted to go to the funeral. Officers warned her to leave the country if she could and certainly to lie low until tensions settled. They even issued her with an official Garda Information Message that her life was in danger, but her grief for her former lover and her loyalty to him seemed to take precedence over common sense or concern for her own safety, and she vowed to attend his funeral ceremony.

Undoubtedly the murder of Lawlor had lowered the imminent threat level for many involved in criminality. Chief Superintendent Christy Mangan recalls:

> That lowered the threat level hugely. The fact that he wasn't going to be directing a certain level of criminal madness dissipated a certain amount of it. We still had the other people involved but they were not at the same level of criminality that he was at and they didn't have the capabilities of getting a gun and deciding they were going to shoot this person and doing it there and then. There are usually assassins for hire, very few carry out these things themselves. We were satisfied we didn't have that type living in Drogheda after Lawlor died. There were a lot of people capable of severe violence but they

didn't have the ability to go out and kill someone. Lawlor's intent was to kill, that is what he brought into Drogheda. He came in there in a rage of pure violence. That volatile nature of his wasn't just about drug taking. There are a lot of people that take drugs and don't kill someone. I think his whole makeup was . . . you just don't see too many of those people in a lifetime and I don't want to see one again. He seemed to just thoroughly enjoy killing people. He knew some of the people that he killed very, very well and it didn't have any effect on him. Whereas I know people who have actually murdered someone and it has a severe psychological effect on them, it tears them apart. They can't deal with it and they end up addicted to substances or tortured throughout their lives. Some commit suicide, they cannot deal with the fact they killed another human being. That wasn't in Robbie Lawlor's DNA. His modus operandi was to inflict as much fear in people, as much violence on them and if that didn't work he would kill you. That is the way he operated. He certainly was a different human being to most of the criminals you would interact with. Thankfully very few operate at the level he operated at.

Another of Lawlor's old associates, Paul Crosby, was also finding that a lifetime of misdeeds was finally catching up with him. Crosby was a top target of gardaí on the anti-Maguire side of the Drogheda feud, the one who rang up his old mentor and mocked him for being in a wheelchair. Witnesses had seen him meeting teenager Keane Mulready-Woods at a Centra shop on the day he disappeared. The last time the 17-year-old was seen alive was in the company of Crosby at the rear of a house where he was later killed and his body dismembered. Just hours after Mulready-Woods' body parts began to show up at various locations throughout Dublin, Crosby had been the target of what's believed to have been a revenge attack when a gunman mistakenly shot an innocent taxi driver who was driving him in rush-hour traffic in Drogheda. The driver had made a good recovery but Crosby, who had been out on bail for other offences, was soon taken off the streets and put in jail after a judge was told he'd breached the terms of his bail on 41 occasions. It was probably the safest place for him to be. Less than three weeks after Lawlor's death, Crosby appeared in court again and received a hefty four and a half-year sentence for his part in the arson of the stolen car on 10 May 2019. In prison he was quizzed about his role in the Keane Mulready-Woods murder.

While the motive for Lawlor's murder was clearly personal grievance, it was ultimately tied up in the desire to earn money and Gardaí knew that the location of the hit in Belfast was more than likely a simple case of opportunity. Lawlor had certainly been in a league of his own and it had always been hard for anyone to see what, if any, was his long-term business plan as he'd terrorised his way through gangland. The fact was that Lawlor had been bad for business and while the celebrations on social media around his death were part of the bravado of the underworld, the reality was that his demise was part of a wider business plan. Mangan explains:

> It is hard to get an understanding of what his long-term business plan was. It seemed to be very scattered. It wouldn't be as

logical as other criminals involved in the drug business. Some of those involved in major distribution of drugs would actually probably succeed in big business because they have a good business brain if that is what you could call it. They have their own ways of controlling the profits and losses which aren't always about inflicting death. It's about dealing with it as a business. Lawlor's whole make-up didn't suit business, he was too volatile to be involved in high-level importations or that level of drug dealing. His nature was always going to cause him major problems and that is what happened in Belfast. If it didn't happen there it would have happened elsewhere because of how he did his business.

Most drug dealers are clever, they don't want to bring attention to themselves, they aren't out and about partying, they aren't driving the big flash cars, they are smart about it. If they are going to do something, they will do it discreetly, they won't leave themselves exposed to the media. There are a lot of people out there who are big-time drug dealers, but the media don't know about them that much or they aren't able to publish what they are at because they have the cover of a business. His behaviour had always caused problems. When two major drug dealing groups fall out there is only gonna be one winner – the Garda Síochána. Fall-outs mean they lose resources and people to prison. When they go to war, and a lot go to prison, the groups start to wane and the power too.

For the Gardaí, Lawlor's murder in Belfast was nothing to do with North–South grievances – it was a simple case of opportunism. They suspected he was working as a debt collector, demanding money with menaces for a number of crime bosses, operating on both sides of the border, but also trying to collect money he believed was owed to his late brother-in-law, Richie Carberry. In the past Belfast might have been a no-go zone for outsiders and a place where drug dealers were policed by paramilitaries, but that was no longer the case. Since the Good Friday Agreement of 1998 things had changed drastically in the criminal underworld. Most Provisionals had hung up their boots, leaving a hardcore element of dissidents who lurched between loose groupings vowing to continue the fight against security forces of the State. While the Real IRA, Continuity IRA and New IRA publicly claimed to be carrying on the work of the Provos by keeping drugs out and fighting for the freedom of their people, in reality most were extorting wealthy drug gangs or working with them. The age-old divide between nationalists and unionists had no place in the new order where powder and pills provided an economy worth fighting for.

Among the gangs vying for control of the drugs market was a notorious narco outfit known as The Firm, which had been linked to murder and drug dealing across County Armagh. It was made up of members from across the community divide, with leading figures from both republican and loyalist backgrounds whose elders had been bitter enemies in the past. Belfast is close to Drogheda and Dublin, particularly northern suburbs like Coolock, and for years supplies had travelled in both directions and business relationships had been cemented. From what gardaí knew, Lawlor was up the North to recover money, a regular activity for him, and he had been travelling to and from

Belfast constantly between January and April. While he was more cautious around Drogheda and north Dublin, he seemed to believe that he was safer in Belfast and hadn't taken as many precautions as he might, even arranging for people to come and see him while he was there and staying regularly in rented Airbnb accommodation. Mangan points out:

> It is not a surprise he is operating in the North. A lot of the Dublin criminals are interacting with the Northern criminals in joint enterprises, be it importation of drugs, firearms, whatever ... The border is not something that impedes them. It is there, in theory, but it is not heavily policed and the checkpoints you had years ago are gone. Nowadays, to nip across the border? It is like going shopping. There is no border. It is an important area for supplying drugs, a market, be it export or import. You've got the port, no more than Dublin port, it is a place where drugs move. We were certainly aware that he had spent a lot of time there in the months before he was killed.

In the run-up to his murder Lawlor had been very active on social media, posting videos of himself enjoying nights out and hinting as to his location in real time. The level of publicity that had surrounded the murder of Keane Mulready-Woods, and especially the political response, had merely made him believe that he was untouchable and someone others needed to fear. In his mind it was good for business and an easy sell to a debtor to pay up quickly, but it was that sense of carefree confidence that had ultimately been his downfall in Belfast. Simply explained,

Lawlor wasn't cautious enough and acts like drinking outside a café bar or socialising in areas that he didn't really know had cost him his life. Mangan said:

> I remember dealing with a seasoned criminal in Dublin years ago and it was coming into October and I asked him how he was and he says 'dreading the winter' – he said he would have to start checking the car in the dark evenings because some bugger was going to try and kill him. And they did try to kill him, but he survived. But that is a person who has survived a number of hits and they are very cagey and cautious getting into their car, they will check for car bombs, to see around the car that there is nobody lurking, they will park their car under a light, they will take all the precautions in the world to make sure they are safe. Robbie, for all his guile and cuteness, he wasn't minding himself the way other criminals would mind themselves, they would be cautious and wouldn't leave themselves exposed, in particular about meeting people, they would keep their back to the wall. It's all the little small things that you do that will ensure that you are gonna live through the next twenty-four hours. It is simple little things like seeing a stranger coming in and wondering who they are. Simple little things. You have to think all the time that there is someone who may have a grievance and is willing to take a pop at you.

Lawlor had travelled to Spain in March, flying out of Belfast International Airport and, ironically, the PSNI suspected that a gunman may have followed him on the flight. While they didn't know if the suspected hitman had aborted plans to kill Lawlor in Spain for a particular reason or simply used the trip as reconnaissance, they did know he had returned more than a week later, picking up a car at the Maldron Hotel and driving towards Newry. They had identified the suspect as a man from Coolock. Lawlor had returned to Belfast via London and then made his way to the South.

The letter to Lawlor's female friend had detailed that he was being actively tracked for weeks in the South and that he had been lucky a number of times. In Belfast it didn't help that he was a loud and unmissable presence on the social scene, in particular around the Cathedral Quarter, but Lawlor was used to not being liked, as long as he was feared – that's all that had mattered to him. That confidence that had built since the murder of Keane Mulready-Woods had left Lawlor blind in other ways and what he hadn't bargained for was that, behind his back, an unholy alliance had formed to take care of him once and for all, one that would criss-cross the island, from Sligo to Limerick, from Dublin to Louth, and right up to where he was in Belfast. Those he once thought of as friends, or at least protectors of sorts, were willing to join forces with his enemies for the common good. People he had double-crossed, people whose friends or associates he had murdered, people who resented his way of doing business and were angry at the public attention his actions had brought down on the underworld. And then those who just believed he had crossed the line with his heinous slaughter of a 17-year-old boy.

Just 15 people showed up at the Sacred Heart Church in Laytown in County Meath to bid farewell to Lawlor at a

Covid-restricted ceremony. His two sisters – Eileen, the widow of Richie Carberry, and Charlene, along with her partner – and Lawlor's brother, his mother Celia and her partner were among the chief mourners. Outside the church a handful of Lawlor's family members and loyal friends stood hooded on the road. Later, he was laid to rest at Dardistown Cemetery in north Dublin, just three graves away from his brother-in-law Richie Carberry. Days later, a young man was knifed when he was jumped on in Marigold Park in Darndale by the same gang who had taken the bag from Robbie Lawlor and sparked his final mad rampage.

On a busy Saturday afternoon on 27 June 2020, less than two months after Lawlor was killed, two gunmen lay in wait outside Warren Crossan's mother's house on St Katherine's Road in Belfast. It was there that Ger Dundon had raced in the Volvo car with a bullet hole in it after, as he'd told police, picking up his nephew Levi Killeen and pal Quincy Bramble from Lawlor's rental flat. Traumatised by his friend Lawlor being killed, he claimed, he then went on to Warren Crossan's home in Crumlin, twenty miles west of Belfast. Crossan had been arrested along with the Dundons, and while he'd yet to be charged in relation to any role the PSNI would claim he played in Lawlor's murder, they were satisfied that he had provided the Scirocco car that, they believed, was a planned getaway vehicle and that was burnt out near the scene of the murder. However, the wheels of justice moved at a slower pace than the word on the streets, where he'd already been named and had his card marked. Hours after his arrest for the Lawlor murder, graffiti had appeared across Belfast naming him as a target. The 28-year-old had ignored the threats and in an act of bravado had told pals he was not worried. But in late June his past caught up with him and he was shot at least five times outside his mother's home in the St James's area of the city. Witnesses to the killing described how he had begged for his life, screaming 'No, no, don't shoot!' as the gun was emptied into him. His killers had arrived on foot, aware that he was a regular visitor at his mother Ann's home. They walked up to him, then chased him onto St Katharine's Road, where they fired the fatal shots before escaping. The fact that no getaway car was involved led cops to conclude that local criminals had to be responsible. Publicly the PSNI refused to rule out the possibility that paramilitaries had acted as guns for hire and that the killers may have lain in wait in a safe house, returning there after their job was done. But whether or not the killing was directly linked to the Lawlor hit was unclear. The way it was carried out and the unusual means of escape by the killers was similar to the modus operandi used by the gunman who had shot drug dealer JD Donegan in December 2018. The flash drug dealer had been sitting behind the wheel of an £80,000 Porsche as he waited to pick up his 13-year-old son from school when he was shot a number of times in the head in broad daylight, with his killer making off on foot into a local housing estate.

Complex gangland relationships appeared to be all over the Lawlor murder and the PSNI found themselves trying to deconstruct a tangled web of intrigue while trying to concentrate on the facts and evidence in the killing. What had become apparent before his death was Crossan's long-standing links to Limerick and to the Dundon brothers. His mother was a Traveller who'd originally come from the same town. Crossan was a high-profile drug dealer and was facing cocaine and motoring charges when he was killed, but Northern politicians were quick to condemn his murder. Sinn Féin's Paul Maskey described it as 'brutal and shameful. My thoughts are with the family of the man who has been killed. No family should have to go through this heartache. Those involved in this act have absolutely no place in our community, they must cease their anti-community activities and get off the back of the people of west Belfast. Those responsible must be held accountable before the courts.' A month later, masked attackers tried to burn down the home Crossan had shared with his partner and young child on Glenfield Close in the village of Crumlin in Antrim, attacking it with petrol bombs in the early hours of the morning.

At the same time the PSNI were beginning to show their hand when it came to the Lawlor murder. Around the same time Crossan was murdered they told a court that Lawlor had been killed by appointment. In Belfast's Magistrates' Court, Adrian Holland had applied for the removal of a bail curfew. During the hearing, evidence was given that he was identified as having met Lawlor on 3 April, the day before he died, at a supermarket car park to hand over cash. Giving evidence, a detective explained that arrangements had been made for a second meeting the following day. 'Robert Lawlor did attend that appointment and when he arrived he was met by a gunman who exited the address and shot him dead in broad daylight. The murder is linked to a feud between organised crime gangs originating out of the Republic of Ireland. It's a comprehensive and complex investigation with numerous links to organised crime gangs operating internationally as well as in mainland UK and throughout Ireland.' Holland had been arrested at his mother's home three days after the murder and later released on bail without charge but with the evening curfew.

At Crossan's funeral at St John's Church on the Falls Road, Belfast, on 3 July, Fr Martin Magill told mourners that Warren had witnessed his father Tommy being gunned down, an event that had scarred him.

> On Good Friday, the eighteenth of April 2014, Warren witnessed his father Tommy being gunned down, an event which traumatised him. Now you, Warren's family, has to deal with this traumatic situation as you've had to deal with Warren's murder on Saturday afternoon ... This local community is known for its generosity, creativity and care. I am confident that you and his family will be supported as you take on this cross of suffering that has come your way. You as Warren's family will carry the cross of a double bereavement, both in horrific circumstances. Parishioners in this parish and beyond Belfast have been praying for you and will continue to pray for you. For you, he was a son, a brother, a partner, a father, an uncle and he was your devoted son who called with you at some point every day or even a number of times each day. For you, Kelly Ann, Debbie, Johnny, Ann and Tommy, he was your beloved brother. And yes, when you stand back and look at it, you had him spoiled. He loved you deeply and became ever more protective of you after the traumatic event of 2014. Georgia, he was your caring partner, he loved, supported and protected you. Thomas, your four years of life meant so much

to your dad. And oh my goodness if he could just see your lovely smile now. And I understand you are a mini version of your dad. Jackson, your birth eight weeks ago gave your dad so much joy, he was there for it. Skin on skin shortly after you arrived into this world with an instant bond of love.

Warren was there for you and his family whenever anything was needed and he went out of his way for you. But you also saw his care for others, the likes of people who were homeless. You've had people in your home, Ann, I know, brought off the streets so they could get cleaned up and [have] somewhere safe to stay for the night. On Saturday afternoon last some of you, Warren's family, saw an evil deed but you also saw acts of kindness. The two gunmen who got up that morning with the intention of executing Warren [in] their deliberate callous way of gunning him down in broad daylight in the presence of neighbours on St Katharine's Road, including children who witnessed it, demonstrated the worst of what human beings can do. I add my voice to those of others calling for people with anything they might have seen or know that would bring to justice those responsible for Warren's murder to bring it forward to the police or to the independent charity, Crimestoppers, which is one hundred per cent anonymous. As well as witnessing this act of evil there were acts of kindness. The neighbour who covered Warren's body with a blanket out of respect for his dead body, another neighbour who covered his face with her headscarf and another who stayed close to his body so that his family knew he had someone with him until his body was removed from the scene. Over these last days you have seen the goodness of human beings.

Despite the pleas for information as Warren Crossan was laid to rest, plans for an audacious and daring crime in his name were under way in the UK, a plot to extort money that would bring to light his close relationship with Ger Dundon, the criminal who'd been caught within hours of Lawlor's murder but released by the PSNI.

On 8 July 2020 two brothers were driven in a BMW car to a flat in Highbury Hill in London, near Arsenal's football stadium. Crossan might have died, but his debts were still very much alive and the two men had been phoned by a man from a number they didn't know and told to go to the flat near the stadium. When they got there, they were greeted by several men, including one who had a handgun tucked into the waistband of his tracksuit bottoms. They were informed a debt they were now responsible for had been increased to £330,000. Another group of men stormed into the apartment, all of them brandishing knives and bladed weapons. The brothers' mobile phones and wallets were taken, and they were pushed to the floor. Their hands were bound with tape and they were blindfolded before being led out of the flat into a waiting vehicle. Over the next week they were moved about until they ended up at halting sites, first in London and later at Smithy Fen in Cambridgeshire, where they were fed sleeping tablets, stripped naked, made to wash with Dettol spray to mask the forensics and given old, dirty clothes to wear. A bucket was provided for 'their basic needs'. The brothers later told police they had believed they were meeting someone to pay a debt of £7,500 for Warren Crossan. The older of the two men had taken on the debt for Crossan, but by the time they were being held hostage it had increased almost fifty-fold. They were threatened with being shot. In one recording of a call made to relatives of the victims, one man was heard saying, 'If you fuck up I'm going to put their brains all over the road, okay. You fuck my people around I'm gonna shoot these two dudes in the head.' The call was made on a phone which had used a fake GPS location setting to scramble where it was coming from.

One of the men was freed on 13 July in the hope that he would get the ransom money for the release of his brother, but unbeknownst to the gang the police had them under surveillance. Three days later a canary yellow Transit van pulled out of the Smithy Fen halting site, but it was stopped by armed police officers only a few hundred metres down the road. There was just one man in the front of the van; he had dark greasy hair and wore a zipped-up navy jacket. Officers observed him trying to damage a mobile phone he was clutching in his hands as they approached the driver's door. Wearing body cameras that filmed the entire interaction, the officers pulled the side door open. Inside they found one man, clearly terrified and disoriented, lying on a mattress with two pillows and a duvet. When quizzed about his passenger in the back of the van, the driver insisted he was his 'mate'. The driver gave his name as Darren McClean. Four more men and a woman were arrested as part of the plot. One was a 34-year-old from Drogheda later described in a CAB case against Owen Maguire and his brother Brendan as a prominent member of the Price–Maguire OCG. The others were Danny Bridges, 41, of Stourport-on-Severn; Lisa Finnerty, 39, of Lancashire; and Quincy Bramble, 33, of East London; along with Cornelius

Price, 41, who was charged with conspiracy to falsely imprison and blackmail the two brothers. The presence of Bramble, who'd been arrested on the day of Lawlor's murder in the company of Ger Dundon and Levi Killeen, along with Cornelius Price, was another sure sign that the men that had been with Lawlor on the day of his killing were crossing both sides. It was an audacious kidnapping, and one that would ultimately lead to the downfall of a new and dangerous figure in the underworld – the man known as Darren McClean.

CHAPTER TEN

The Case against the Alleged Killers

In December 2020 Adrian Holland, 37, and Patrick Teer, 45, appeared in Belfast Magistrates' Court charged with the murder of Robbie Lawlor. The pair knew one another but both steadfastly denied they had anything to do with the killing. Both appeared remotely, and despite the threat to their lives they were seeking to be released from custody; they were particularly concerned given the length of time they could remain in prison awaiting trial. Covid had left a backlog of cases in an already grinding system in Northern Ireland and they were likely to spend two or three years in prison before their case could get under way. During the course of the bail hearing a judge was told that the evidence against them was based on number plate recognition and cell site analysis, a method of identifying where a mobile phone is at a specific time by using 'pings' from mobile phone masts. Most significantly, the court was told, the hit on Lawlor had been organised in Sligo, and Holland had travelled there to meet an international drug dealer, while Teer had paid for his stay. The court also heard that it was the Crown's case that the pair had liaised after the killing in order to 'get their stories straight'.

Sligo, on Ireland's north-east corner, was not the most likely place to plan Lawlor's killing, given its distance from both north Dublin and Drogheda, where his most significant enemies were living and operating. However, for a country town on Ireland's western seaboard, Sligo had seen its fair share of gangland activity. Its proximity to the border and violent and connected groupings had put it on the map. Since the turn of the century there had been a war for control which at one point only allowed one grouping to reign supreme. The growth of cocaine had meant that by the time Robbie Lawlor was shot dead, Sligo had four major groupings and was being tackled pre-emptively by special Garda operations to prevent it becoming the next Drogheda.

Despite there being more than twenty suspects identified as part of the investigation into the gangster's death, just Teer and Holland had been charged. Neither was suspected of being the gunman; they were both facing charges of joint enterprise with unidentified others. The court had been told that international drug dealers were believed to have been involved in planning Lawlor's assassination and credible threats were made against anyone thinking about helping with the police investigation. At Belfast's Magistrates' Court a detective inspector went through the details of the case they had pieced together so far, and how they believed Lawlor was shot dead after travelling to a pre-arranged meeting at the house in Ardoyne owned by Adrian Holland's family. When he got there a gunman came out of the front door, opened fire and shot Lawlor several times, the court was told. He died at the scene but the gunman fled down several side streets to where a stolen Volkswagen Scirocco was supposed to be waiting for him to use as a getaway car. But it had been set on fire. Instead, an Audi vehicle, which was later found, also burnt out, in the Crumlin area of the city, was believed to have been used in the gunman's escape. The court heard how Patrick Teer was allegedly 'instrumental' in moving the getaway cars for the man who shot Lawlor into the Ardoyne area on 31 March. Mobile phone evidence also showed that Teer had been tracking Robbie Lawlor and his movements in the days before he was shot. 'The case against Mr Teer is that he was specifically involved in research, logistics, disposal and the interference with the course of justice,' a police detective explained to the court.

Adrian Holland and Barry Young, who was not named in court but who was described as an international drug dealer, had met at the Sligo Park Hotel in March, the PSNI stated, and that trip was organised and paid for by Teer, they claimed. After the murder, the police further alleged, Teer met up with Holland to arrange their story and organise a forensic 'clean-up'. The detective continued, 'Throughout the course of this period in terms of planning, preparation and execution of the murder, Patrick Teer is in contact not only with Adrian Holland but also some international drug dealers and members of a very significant organised crime gang. Ultimately it's our view that Mr Teer has been instrumental in this murder, and without his involvement it couldn't have happened.' Teer's defence barrister, however, said the entire case against his client boiled down to his association with Adrian Holland – a man who grew up in a neighbouring street. 'When you consider his own circumstances, particularly the fact he's driving his own car, bringing Mr Holland places and allowing his phone to be used, it's actually absurd to suggest he knowingly had anything to do with this,' the lawyer said. His bail was denied.

Building the case against Teer and Holland had brought officers back to Robbie Lawlor's activities in the North from at least January, when he had begun visiting Belfast frequently. They suspected that since the murder of his brother-in-law, Richie Carberry, Lawlor had been keeping the wolf from the door by trying to collect funds he believed were owed to Carberry before he died; he had told friends that at least £400,000 was owed to him. In their investigation into the murder of Robbie Lawlor, PSNI investigators had attempted to track vehicles from late January as they moved through Enniskillen and crossed the border into Sligo. Phone coverage showed that Lawlor had travelled from Belfast to Spain in early March and that the suspected gunman had followed him there. Whether it was intended to kill him in Spain or if it was simply a reconnaissance mission was unclear.

Lines of enquiry had brought investigators from the North into the South, where gardaí had gathered CCTV footage from 16 March at the hotel in Sligo where Holland had stayed for a number of nights. On that afternoon he'd been spotted at reception before making his way to the foyer. An Audi saloon believed to belong to Barry Young had driven into the car park and grainy footage suggested the two had spoken before parting ways. The investigation had tracked Lawlor travelling north in the days that followed and Holland visiting Sligo and remaining in contact with Young. PSNI officers had tracked a number of suspect cars moving about Belfast. On 1 April, CCTV had captured images of three men meeting on University Road in Belfast, near where Lawlor had been staying. They had been identified as Lawlor, Ger Dundon and Levi Killeen. They had left the Tesco car park and later that evening another image captured Dundon with Bramble. The PSNI had identified an apartment on the same road where Lawlor was staying that had been rented through Airbnb. That same night Dundun, Killeen and Bramble were seen leaving the apartment and driving a blue Volvo car. The mobile phone investigation had found that a number of significant players from Belfast and Donegal were in touch on their phones throughout the next 72 hours and in the run-up to Lawlor's murder. On 3 April, the day before he was killed, the VW Scirocco was parked up in Estoril Park before 10am. That day there was another meeting in Tesco about 5pm; this was the gathering the PSNI had referred to in their evidence to the court. As the case was built the PSNI created a picture of up to 20 people circling the prey.

In mid-May 2021 Paul Crosby and Gerard Cruise, both of Rathmullan Park in Drogheda, were arrested and charged with the murder of 17-year-old Keane Mulready-Woods. By the end of the month it was ruled that their case would be heard in the non-jury Special Criminal Court. In certain cases, the Director of Public Prosecutions can certify that in their opinion the ordinary courts are inadequate to secure the effective administration of justice. In other words, there's a possible risk of jury tampering or intimidation. Crosby was already in custody, having been jailed for four years for arson of a stolen car, which had happened while he was under Garda surveillance for involvement in feud activities alongside Robbie Lawlor.

In November 2021, Gerard 'Ged' McKenna pleaded guilty to cleaning up and removing evidence from his home in Rathmullan Park, the house where Keane Mulready-Woods was murdered. The court heard that it was not suggested that the dad of eight had been present when the youngster was killed or during the 'shocking dismemberment of the boy'. Later, during sentence hearing, Detective Sergeant Peter Cooney was taken through the facts of the case by prosecuting counsel Michael Delaney SC. Cooney said he'd got a warrant to search McKenna's house on foot of confidential information. When gardaí entered it at 4.50pm on 14 January, he said, they noticed a strong smell of paint. A technical examination found that bloodstaining was visible and forensic examination found Keane Mulready-Woods' blood at different locations in the house, including along the ceilings and walls, under the front window, on the leg of the TV table, on the Sky box and at the fireplace. The detective sergeant said a number of items were recovered from a fire in a green area near the property, including a ballistic vest and a box of penknives, which both had Keane's blood on them. Keys to a car were found in the property and when it was searched more items with the teenager's blood on them were found, including an axe handle, socks and a bone fragment.

McKenna was arrested on 20 February. During the interview, he said he'd returned home that day and 'didn't recognise the place' as it had been cleaned. He said he was told to 'burn the bags' but didn't know what was in them. Phone records were shown to McKenna during the interview, including calls from Robbie Lawlor. McKenna had told gardaí, 'He will kill my child . . . I don't know why I took the call.' The court heard that McKenna had met a number of men in a café in West Street in Drogheda on 12 January that year and had stayed in a friend's house that night. He brought a packet of pink pills and the court heard he was 'talking funny' and said 'I could have been down there, cut up.' McKenna, the court heard, had bought a pot of paint and taken another pot of paint and three pallets of wooden flooring from his friend's home. When he was arrested he took an overdose of prescription drugs in the garda station and spent three days in hospital. He told gardaí he had been told to stay away from the house and had carried out his instructions under duress. He was 'off his head' when involved in the clean-up and was ashamed of what he had done, he said. Sentencing him to four years in prison, Mr Justice Paul McDermott said that while McKenna had expressed shame about his involvement, and had known the youngster since he was born, he still 'surrendered' his home to an organised criminal gang. 'Turning a blind eye and assisting criminal gangs is the essential bedrock of their success and this kind of assistance must be discouraged,' the judge said. The court heard that the person who ordered McKenna to surrender his house was 'a person of very significant notoriety, with a number of murders attributed to him'. And that this person, who we now know was Robbie Lawlor, 'was not easy to say no to and when they tell you to do something you do it.'

In early December 2022 Crosby pleaded guilty at the Special Criminal Court to the lesser charge of facilitating Keane Mulready-Woods' murder. Gerard Cruise's lawyers told the court that day that their client would do the same. (Months later, in the middle of the Regency trial, which saw the legendary criminal Gerry 'The Monk' Hutch stand accused of the murder of David Byrne at the Regency Hotel, a crime that had sparked a huge backlash of murder against the Hutch OCG and innocent members of the Hutch family, they were sentenced to ten and seven years respectively.) In court Crosby smiled and tried to joke with journalists packed into the courtroom to hear evidence around the Regency Hotel event. He was aged just 27, and had been only 25 at the time of Keane Mulready-Woods' murder. After he was arrested, Cruise had admitted to gardaí that he had dropped Mulready-Woods and Crosby to McKenna's house. He said everything seemed fine between the teenager and Crosby and he did not know what was to happen at the house. The Special Criminal Court also heard that Crosby had 40 previous convictions, including for road traffic offences, possession of drugs, criminal damage, theft and fraud, and arson. While serving time in prison he was convicted of being in possession of a mobile phone. Crosby had also been previously acquitted of attempted murder in February 2019 when he had been accused of trying to kill Gerard Boyle at Beauparc, near Slane, County Meath on 10 November 2016. (Mr Boyle had been stabbed 28 times and forced into the boot of a car, which was then pushed into a canal.) Crosby's barrister, Michael Bowman SC, said Crosby had had difficulties with cocaine from a young age but was now abstaining from drugs.

The victim's mother, Elizabeth Woods, in a victim impact statement described her son's murder as 'inhumane, violent and a barbaric death'. She said it was 'one of the most brutal, tragic and horrifying murders in the history of Ireland' and she hoped no other family would go through what her family had. She recalled the two burials for her son as his body parts were found at different times in different areas of the country. On his birthday, she said, the family brought cake to his grave. 'Keane would never mind what presents he got as long as he had a nice cake.' She said she heard him call to her and battled every day with knowing she couldn't help her son. 'The haunting nightmares will live with us for ever. The loss is something we will have to live with. You don't get over it, you don't move on.' Mr Justice Tony Hunt told the court how the circumstances around the teenager's murder had fed into the gravity of the offences committed by both Crosby and Cruise. 'It is painful and unnatural to lose a child prematurely,' he said. 'But it is particularly so when it comes about as a result of the crime of murder. In this case the remains of the child were treated in a disgraceful and inhuman way that beggars belief.' The judge also detailed how the chief suspect for the murder was Robbie Lawlor, a criminal of 'significant notoriety and linked to several murders' who was heavily involved in a feud between rival criminal gangs in Drogheda. Such gangs, the judge said, were the 'scourge of the localities concerned and are a matter of nationwide concern.'

Back in the UK police were still trying to get a trial date for the kidnapping of the two brothers who held the Warren Crossan debt. But what, on the face of it, seemed an ordinary case of extortion in the criminal underworld was set to become a stage for the ever-more intricate relationships and fate of those whose worlds had collided with Robbie Lawlor. In December 2021, at London's Wood Green Crown Court, the case was adjourned when the judge was told that one of the defendants, Cornelius Price, was in a coma and that doctors were unsure when he might wake up. It was a shocking diagnosis, and nothing to do with his life of crime; just one of those cards that life can deal you sometimes. Price had been struck down with limbic encephalitis, an illness in which areas of the brain are swollen and stop working properly, affecting memory, learning, and emotions such as aggression. The condition can also leave sufferers susceptible to seizures. As Price's lawyer told the court: 'He has been in the hospital for quite some time now. He is still ventilated at the moment. In terms of his ongoing treatment and diagnosis, the consultant said that it is difficult to estimate when Price is likely to wake from his coma. It could be months or the worst-case scenario is it could be years.' Gravely ill in a Welsh hospital, Price would not be able to stand trial with his five alleged associates; Danny Bridges, Mark Kavanagh, Quincy Jarron Bramble, Lisa Marie Finnerty and the previously unknown Darren McClean, the man caught red-handed driving the canary yellow van.

CHAPTER ELEVEN

'It's a very, very, very good theory, your honour'

Joe Brolly had always done good drama. Loved and loathed by the public in equal measure, over the years he delighted and infuriated sports fans with his boisterous contributions as a pundit on RTÉ's *The Sunday Game*. In late 2022, with his GAA hat off and his barrister's gown firmly on, he proved that he wasn't all that different in a courtroom. Instructed by solicitor Ciaran Shiels of Madden and Finucane solicitors, Brolly got to his feet, first at Belfast's Magistrates' Court and later in the High Court representing Adrian Holland, and dramatically stated: 'I smell a rat in this case. I've smelt a rat from the outset.' While it is usually up to the prosecution to detail a vivid picture of how a murder plays out and who pulled the trigger, Brolly took it upon himself to tell the court what the defence team's theory was in the case of who killed Robbie Lawlor. With his usual theatrical flair, Brolly told Mr Justice O'Hara:

> Up until this application the defence have been at the disadvantage that we've not been able to see the papers to understand

precisely what the case is. We say that it is now clear that there is a real doubt about whether or not this accused was aware that a murder was going to take place, never mind participating in it. Don't forget that it is accepted that he was not the gunman, nor was he part of the hit team . . . this is now a dubious case and there are gaps in the case which we say, having read the evidence, that the prosecution are not able to close. We say that the prosecution case, in essence, is a vague one that doesn't make particular sense.

Brolly pointed to the interviews of Holland, in particular those conducted in the December after the murder, during which, he said, his client was told by officers, 'You are some way mixed up in this – do you want to tell us what you know so we can exonerate you?' Brolly told the judge that during the interviews Holland was told that he had gone to the Crumlin area of Belfast on the night before the murder, where he had met with Ger Dundon and Robbie Lawlor. He told the judge that the defence case was that this meeting was the first time Holland had met Dundon, although he knew Lawlor and was friends with him for months.

He also set out a bizarre set of circumstances: after his arrest Holland was represented by a man claiming to be a solicitor but who was in fact a teacher who was the life partner of a lawyer and who misrepresented himself to both his client and the PSNI. Should Holland not have been told by the fake solicitor to say nothing, Brolly contended, he would have given an account which would have exonerated him during those early interviews and would have been a witness rather than an accused in the case. The barrister went on to detail how Holland was interviewed five times on 8 April 2020, four days after the murder. He'd presented himself voluntarily and had no solicitor present but had phone contact between interviews with the 'gentleman' (whose name was given in a note to the judge) who had claimed to be a solicitor. 'The applicant (Holland) believed he was a solicitor but he was not a solicitor. He was to our clear and certain knowledge a school teacher, the life partner of the solicitor in the case and who also had represented himself to all and sundry as a solicitor when he was not.' Brolly said that on 8 December 2020, when Holland had come back for an interview, the same man had appeared remotely by Facetime and told police that his client would not be answering any questions. 'Why are you interviewing him? Why are you continuing to waste our time? That was the constant message,' said Brolly. The 'solicitor', the court heard, had arrived at Etna Drive on the morning of the murder and had introduced himself to police as Adrian Holland's solicitor and had told them that his client was involved in drugs offences and criminality and that if he had been murdered it would not be a surprise. 'It beggars belief. You couldn't make it up, my lord,' Brolly said with dramatic effect. The 'solicitor' had said he first met Holland in Maghaberry Prison, having been introduced to him by his lifelong friend, the co-accused Patrick Teer. 'Adrian Holland had contacted Patrick from the prison asking for his help to find a new solicitor,' explained Brolly, who said the 'solicitor' attended at the prison and signed Holland up as a 'client' for his practice. At Etna Drive he asked if it was

Holland who'd been shot, saying he'd received phone calls to that effect. 'During the interview process he told Holland to keep his mouth shut. He told him that MI5 had it all on camera and that he had nothing to worry about and to say nothing and he'd walk,' said Brolly. 'Inevitable an application to exclude his interviews will be successful. So we say this was a man who could have given an innocent explanation had he not been told not to say anything.' He told the court that the decision to charge Holland was 'impacted by the course advised by this "solicitor" throughout'.

It was only in the corridor outside the court on the day Holland was charged, 10 December 2020, that it emerged that the man was not a solicitor. 'He was there, suit on, briefcase in hand,' Brolly said. Focusing on the harder evidence of the case, Brolly described the PSNI investigation into the Lawlor murder as 'flawed'. 'I do not make that allegation lightly and will ground it with clear and compelling evidence,' he said. He went on to point to the then ongoing prosecution in the Central Criminal Court in Dublin of four people related to two organised crime gangs from Dundalk and Limerick, who, he said, 'planned and carried out this murder'. Brolly was referring to the case against Ciara Lynch and her co-accused Kathleen O'Reilly, associates of the Dundon crime family.

> The defence in this case has been given the four hundred-page book of evidence from that case. The applicant is not so much as mentioned, nor has been Teer. The background is that the deceased, Robbie Lawlor, is believed to have shot Owen

Maguire, the head of the Maguire family in Drogheda, paralysing him from the neck down. He was also the suspected gunman in the murder of Kenneth Finn and David Lynch. The Gardaí arrested and interviewed and released him in relation to those. In January 2020 Keane Mulready-Woods was murdered in a gruesome attack in which he was decapitated and a flip-flop was put in his mouth.

At this point an irritated Justice O'Hara stopped Brolly and said, 'What do you not get about me? I'm not a jury, you don't need to dress things up.' Brolly said he had simply wanted to lay out the feud background as it had nothing to do with his client Adrian Holland, who had no animosity against the deceased Robbie Lawlor. But taking his lead from the judge, Brolly moved swiftly to the point of his address to the court.

> They'd [Holland and Lawlor] known each other for several months, he had absolutely zero animus towards him and the known evidence is that Ger Dundon drove Mr Lawlor to the scene and it had to have been pre-planned by Dundon. As soon as Lawlor got out of the car a gunman, believed to be Levi Killeen, the son of John Dundon and a member of the McCarthy–Dundon crime gang, approaches on foot and shoots him dead. Ger Dundon is left unharmed and this caused the PSNI eyebrows to raise initially. Then Ger Dundon, Levi Killeen and Quincy Bramble, who is described as a dark-coloured person and who is another notorious hitman and member of the Dundon–McCarthy gang, were arrested leaving Belfast shortly after the murder.

Brolly continued:

> So Dundon is on his own and Lawlor gets out. He is assassinated and Dundon is left unharmed. Two cars are burnt out. We say the car that Levi Killeen was in and the getaway car were burnt out. Dundon then picks the two men up and then all three are intercepted leaving Belfast. We know because of our interviews which they had to disclose to us that all three were questioned by the PSNI and for unknown reasons released without charge or follow-up. We have been refused all requests for disclosure of their interviews and of the circumstances of their interviews.

Brolly went on to describe a scenario that he said he and Mr Shiels had discussed numerous times and at length.

> Bear in mind Levi Killeen has never seen nor met Robbie Lawlor. This is a CCTV viewing record from the first of April, three days before the murder, at Tesco Express on University Road. Robbie Lawlor's flat is above the Tesco Express where the CCTV is. My Lord will see two males walk left to right. The first is Ger Dundon and the second is Quincy Bramble, a black male in a peaked cap. Both walk to the apartment entrance and enter. That's Robbie Lawlor's apartment. The male who was the passenger in the black Mercedes is on foot and that is Levi Killeen Then see that twenty-four minutes later three people cross the road on foot. That is Ger Dundon, Levi Killeen and Quincy Bramble. Killeen is carrying a back bag. Then a saloon car passes and Dundon and Bramble make sure Killeen gets a

look at Lawlor. Killeen hangs back, giving the gunman a look at Robert Lawlor.

The judge looked at Brolly: 'That is your theory?' he asked. 'It's a very good theory, it's a very, very, very good theory, Your Honour. I cannot think of another explanation,' the barrister responded. 'We say that the case against the accused is perilously weak and it is based on assumptions and speculation . . . Lo and behold, on the morning of the murder, and we know because the police put it in interviews, that Ger Dundon picks up Robbie Lawlor at his apartment and drives him up to the location and as soon as he gets out he is murdered. The gunman, we say, is Levi Killeen. Ger Dundon picks him up and they drive together before being intercepted coming out of Belfast.'

Brolly returned again to the case in the South related to the days after the murder when Francis Maguire and Simon McGinley drove from Drogheda under Garda surveillance to the car park of the Maldron Hotel in Portlaoise to meet with Ciara Lynch and Kathleen O'Reilly. 'Gardaí move in and intercept it and there is fifty K in cash. This is the payment from the Maguire OCG to Dundon OCG for the successful assassination of Robbie Lawlor,' he told the court. He went on to tell the judge that in Garda interviews it was put to each accused if the money was payment for the Robbie Lawlor murder. 'And it makes perfect sense,' the barrister said. 'A case which is centred and plausible: scouting it out three days earlier, the three intercepted leaving Belfast, Ger Dundon delivering him to the scene, the Maguires pay the Dundons the following day with fifty thousand euros in cash. And the PSNI release all three of them?'

The High Court case also revealed that the PSNI had put it to Holland under questioning that Dundon had told them a meeting had been arranged at his house in Etna Drive and that Dundon admitted he was bringing Lawlor to the meeting. Brolly said:

> Clearly that was lies. He was lying his way out of the situation when it was Dundon with Maguire that clearly engineered this murder ... Police say Robbie Lawlor and Ger Dundon are two big names in the criminal gangs in Ireland, well connected and with access to firearms and drugs, nutters who go around murdering people. Robbie Lawlor was wanted dead and we suspect he was wanted dead by a lot of people, certainly in the South of Ireland and indeed across the water. Dundon thought, 'happy days, he is a mug, we'll get him set up at his house.'

Brolly told the court that the defence would say that once focus had been placed on Holland and Teer by the PSNI the case had become skewed, but there was no motive. In the case of Holland he had no story, he said; he didn't flee the area following the murder and he left a trail that led straight back to him. An aunt of Holland, he told the court, had told the PSNI that the key was always in the back door of 61 Etna Drive and that the front door was always unlocked. He said family members had told officers he was in an aunt's house nearby when news came that someone had been shot. They said Holland had jumped up and was shaking and immediately made himself available to police. 'He was scared, jittery, and receptive to the PSNI being with him, he co-operated fully,' he told the court. He also referred to the fact that Holland had gone to Sligo in the aftermath of the murder but had left his number with police. He said the three Dundon men had been 'airbrushed' from the papers given to defence.

The court heard how Holland was on bail at the time of the murder after a weapon had been found in the dog house in the rear yard of the house. The gun, Brolly said, was a 105-year-old Webley Colt. It had been examined by forensic scientists and had to be cleaned and oiled before it would function; the cartridges in the chamber were in such poor condition that they were incapable of discharge. Counsel for the State said that the investigation into the murder of Robbie Lawlor was not yet complete and while a file in respect of Teer and Holland was ready, there were still other individuals at large. Counsel repeated that the PSNI believed over twenty people were still being actively considered as having had a role in the murder. But the State doubled down on its belief that the Dundon grouping had nothing whatsoever to do with Lawlor's murder. Counsel concluded:

> I would set out that the three individuals that Mr Brolly has referred to and firmly pointed the finger at were considered at the outset as the PSNI would be expected to do. But the prosecution can confirm that there is no evidence that supports Dundon, Killeen and Bramble as being involved in the murder. In fact, material points away from that suggestion. I appreciate that might be one theory but not a theory the prosecution considers and evidence points away from that. We have no duty to disclose that evidence at this point.

In relation to the cash handover, the Crown said that Gardaí were solely investigating money-laundering and therefore would not have included the activities of Teer or Holland in their line of questioning to the suspect. 'In relation to Ger Dundon it is correct to say he was physically unharmed but the vehicle he had driven was shot at and did have a bullet mark in it.' Asked by the judge if Dundon and Lawlor were both targets, the prosecution conceded that they could not go that far.

While Dundon might have dodged a bullet in Belfast (according to the State), or escaped a murder rap because of PSNI incompetence (according to Brolly), his luck was about to run out in the UK, where he had fled in the aftermath of the Lawlor murder. As the kidnap trial of Cornelius Price and his five accomplices continued to make its way through the courts, albeit with the mob boss still critically ill in hospital, it emerged that the defendant known as Darren McClean was actually Ger Dundon. With his brothers Wayne, John and Dessie serving life sentences for murder, Ger had fared better than his siblings and had received just short sentences for crimes over the decades, the latest being in October 2018 when he'd been given just four years by the Special Criminal Court for helping to hide a sawn-off automatic pump-action shotgun. With remission and time served he'd been released from prison a year later and had moved between the UK and Ireland ever since. What emerged during the kidnap case in the UK was that he'd also changed his name by deed poll to Darren McClean and registered his age on official documents as three years younger than he was. His long rap sheet and the ability to travel without the notorious Dundon name was behind his decision to hide his real identity.

After the Lawlor murder, Dundon had moved to the UK, where he'd immediately hooked up with Cornelius Price, a chief suspect in the complicated Belfast killing. The relationship with Price was a business one, a joint enterprise in organised crime, undoubtedly rooted in their Traveller backgrounds, but his presence with the mob boss when they were nabbed in the kidnap plot gave strength to the Brolly theory that the Maguire and Price organisations were working with the Dundon OCG around the time of the Lawlor murder. Not only had money changed hands in the days after the murder, but the UK case proved that Ger Dundon was operating hand in glove with one of Lawlor's sworn enemies, Cornelius Price. Gravely ill in a Welsh hospital, the chances of Price ever standing trial for the kidnap seemed less likely as the months went on and the case was put on ice pending medical news about his condition.

A new date in November 2022 was eventually fixed for the trial to go ahead with Price on bail and fitted with an electronic tag in his hospital bed. He had been charged with kidnap and blackmail charges along with Mark Kavanagh from Drogheda, who was listed as a member of the Maguire OCG. McClean, aka Dundon, and Bramble, who'd been with him in Belfast when Lawlor was murdered, were both facing kidnap charges. Danny Bridges and Lisa Finnerty were charged with conspiracy to unlawfully imprison the two men against their will. All six had pleaded not guilty and Dundon/McClean had secured bail due to pressure on the UK prison system during the coronavirus pandemic. But he'd quickly gone back to his old ways and had attacked a man, stolen an electric bike and committed other offences, so his bail was revoked.

When the case was eventually heard, evidence was given that Crossan owed a debt which the accused men believed had been inherited by the businessman who was held captive with his brother. The businessman had declined to tell police about the money or his connection with the murdered Crossan. The prosecution laid out their case that McClean and Bramble had kidnapped the brothers; Price and Bridges had made menacing phone calls demanding the ransom to be paid for their release; and Finnerty had conspired with the others when they went to collect the ransom. Another man described as 'Skinny Irish' by the brothers had a Northern Irish accent but was never apprehended or identified. Prosecutor Anne Whyte QC told the jury:

> The victims were kidnapped without warning on the eighth of July 2020 in north London. Darren McClean and Quincy Bramble were directly involved in and responsible for that kidnapping. Each defendant in this case then conspired with each other and with others, not present in this court, to falsely imprison and to blackmail the victims with a view to extracting cash and/or other commodities including drugs from them after they had been kidnapped.

She said that the victims were driven to the flat near Arsenal football stadium in a hired BMW car:

> Some of the men in the flat were armed. McClean was wearing jogging bottoms, a jacket and a facemask. The victim could see a handgun in McClean's waistband. Inside the flat, McClean spoke to the victims. Then without warning four or five men stormed into the room. They were all armed with

knives or bladed weapons. The victims were pushed to the floor and told not to move. Mobile phones and wallets were taken from them. Between them they were carrying over £2,000 in cash. The car keys to the BMW were also taken . . . They were held against their will to different locations and blackmailed. On occasion, they were threatened with weapons, bound and at times blindfolded. Soon after being kidnapped in London they were moved by car to a place called Smithy Fen, a Travellers' site north of Cambridge. There they were both held captive.

Near the upmarket village of Cottenham in Cambridgeshire, Smithy Fen had gained a reputation as a massive illegal Traveller site. In 2002 hundreds of Travellers began to descend on the picturesque area and set up permanent homes there. A year later an estimated 800 Irish Travellers joined them, turning the site into a 20-acre settlement without planning permission. A lengthy battle with local residents and the council followed before bulldozers moved in to clear a number of pitches, leaving more than fifty other settlements. Over the years, members of the notorious Rathkeale Rovers crime gang – the group who were investigated over a major plot to steal rhino horn and Chinese artefacts in a series of museum raids – had given addresses at Smithy Fen.

On the Smithy Fen site, the gang agitated for money, the court was told. 'Over the days that followed, demands were made for a large sum of money to secure their release. The scale of the demands would vary from day to days but at times were as high as over £300,000. Both victims were held captive together at

Smithy Fen until the thirteenth of July.' Two phones had been used to make the demands, the prosecution claimed, and a friend of one of the victims delivered boxes to a Starbucks car park near Stoke-on-Trent, where he gave them to Finnerty, who drove to the Stourport home address of Cornelius Price. The following day Finnerty drove back to the Price residence, the court heard, and then on to London. On that day McClean and Bramble drove the second victim from Smithy Fen to London, where he was given money and one of his phones and told to go home and help raise more money. The first victim continued to be held captive at Smithy Fen until McClean was arrested in the canary yellow van. During the course of their captivity the victims had been washed with Dettol and threatened.

The conniving nature of McClean/Dundon emerged during the case when a police officer said that when under arrest he had claimed that he had become aware that the victim had been robbed in London and that he had been contacted by a mutual friend to help him out. He said he was told to meet at a flat in London where the victim told him he needed money urgently. He claimed he stayed with the brothers for around four days in total and said neither was held against his will and no money was ever demanded. He claimed one slept in the back of his van by choice, and that both were 'pretending' to be kidnapped. He said it was all a plan by one of the victims to get money from people he knew so he could pay a debt.

When the court returned its verdicts, just McClean was convicted of conspiracy to kidnap one of the two brothers as well as conspiring to blackmail both men. His co-accused were acquitted on all charges. 'This is bullshit! This court is corrupt to the backbone!' he shouted when the jury delivered its verdict at Wood Green. Dundon/McClean was shocked by the guilty verdicts. Earlier he'd been found not guilty of kidnapping the brothers and not guilty of conspiring to falsely imprison one, and it looked like he, as well as Bramble, would walk free. In the body of the court Kenneth Dundon Sr, dressed in a full Peaky Blinders-style suit, stood up and stormed out. As Judge Dodd finished his summation his son shouted: 'Tell Dad I'm alright. I'm alright, Da.'

Dundon Sr was no stranger to where his son was headed. Since his violent offspring had returned to Limerick twenty years before, when Wayne was deported from the UK by order of the Home Office, dad Kenneth had lived a chaotic and violent existence. He was handed down a six-year manslaughter sentence in 2006 for stabbing Christopher Jacobs, who he believed was having an affair with his now late wife Anne at a London flat. Dundon had fled the UK after stabbing his victim in the face. He'd been arrested for the crime but was released on bail and returned to Limerick, making Irish legal history when he became the first person arrested and extradited under an EU warrant. Back in the UK he'd pleaded guilty to manslaughter. The court heard that Anne McCarthy had begun a sexual relationship with Jacobs, a heroin user, after meeting him at a Department of Social Services office in 2003. Kenneth Dundon became angry that his wife was regularly spending nights away from their home and after a number of altercations donned a mask, kicked in Jacobs's door and attacked him. Jacobs had choked to death on his own blood as Dundon fled. Following his release Dundon had attended son John's murder trial and had moved between Limerick and the UK ever since.

While Ger Dundon was returned to custody pending sentencing his co-accused were free to go where they wished and headed straight to the pub to celebrate their victory. Kavanagh had been described by a senior investigator, in an affidavit filed with the High Court as part of a CAB case against mob boss Owen Maguire and his brother Brendan, as 'a prominent member of the Price-Maguire OCG.' He had fled to the UK in 2020 in the aftermath of the Keane Mulready-Woods murder, but with 27 previous convictions and two live warrants for his arrest was unlikely to return to Drogheda.

Within months of Ger Dundon's conviction, and as he awaited sentence from a UK court, Cornelius Price succumbed to his illness. Just hours after he died tributes were posted online including a last-minute conversion he was said to have had with the support of a Christian preacher. Videos of the last moments of his life showed members of the Price family gathered around his hospital bed, where he was intubated, at Cwmbran in Wales. But the tables were soon turned on the criminal who'd toasted Robbie Lawlor's death with a glass of Captain Morgan rum, when rivals used the videos to gloat over his death. They used the footage of Price during his last moments as a backdrop for a crude final farewell. Later, in Rochdale in Greater Manchester, three Lamborghinis, yellow, maroon and white, led the funeral cortège of mourners wearing specially printed T-shirts bearing Price's image to a cemetery covered in lavish floral tributes in which he was described as 'king', 'golden balls' and 'legend'. Four barriers with red velvet rope surrounded the grave, with arrangements depicting Captain Morgan rum, a bottle of mayonnaise and a mocked-up front page of the *Sunday World* newspaper. Absent from the gathering was paralysed mob boss Owen Maguire, who believed he could be arrested by UK police if he attended, over an assault in a pub in Manchester back in 2017. Instead he posted tributes to his pal online.

By May Ger Dundon had been told he'd serve a 15-year sentence for his role in the kidnap and for firearms offences, the longest jail term he'd ever received. Sentencing the Limerick mobster, Judge John Dodds recommended he serve at least half of the sentence before he could be considered for release. Deputy senior investigating officer Detective Sergeant Garry Jackson of Staffordshire Police said the experience of the two kidnapped brothers had been 'terrifying'. 'It also had a profound impact on their family members and friends. The investigation was incredibly complex and involved a number of police forces who supported our efforts, including the Metropolitan Police and Cambridgeshire Constabulary. We are pleased that McClean [Dundon] will now be serving a substantial sentence which reflects the seriousness of this disturbing crime.'

CHAPTER TWELVE

The Sligo Connection

For its size, Sligo, with a population of just over 20,000 in the town and a little more than 70,000 in the county, had always punched above its weight when it came to gangland activity. Famed as the home of poet WB Yeats, Sligo offers culture and history to tourists, but under the surface it had long been a key location as a rural underworld headquarters.

Since the early 2000s two groupings had stood out in the town, one a Traveller mob and the second a family from the centre of the town known as the Irwins. Headed up by eldest brother Hughie Irwin, the familial group had gone to war with the McGinleys and in 2005, Hughie McGinley was gunned down in broad daylight by the pillion passenger on a motorbike as he sat in a van on a busy Sligo street. That year was marked by feud murders in Dublin gang wars involving the notorious Westies mob in Blanchardstown, the rival groups of Brian Rattigan and 'Fat' Freddie Thompson in Crumlin, and murders ordered by the notorious Martin 'Marlo' Hyland in Finglas. While specialist units were focused on the bigger feuds, Sligo detectives were left to deal with their own problems. Hughie Irwin was arrested and quizzed about the murder but he spread excrement on his face during his custody period and later left Ireland for Lanzarote, leaving the day-to-day running of the business to his younger brother Patrick. Patrick went on to earn himself the title of a west of Ireland King Scum when he tried to introduce heroin to the town. A Lothario, he'd been considered one of the most dangerous mobsters in the country when he became a close associate of Eamon 'The Don' Dunne and Limerick godfather Brian Collopy, making him the first criminal from the north-west to forge links with other powerful gangs. The wheels came off his criminal empire in March 2008 when Gardaí launched Operation Golf, spearheaded by CAB, which saw 19 addresses searched, including one on Lough Gill. At the time officers believed the Irwin group were using the remote island to store drugs and cash and had been using a boat to ferry the loads across. The mid-noughties was a boom time for cocaine and it had started to become the recreational drug of choice across the country. Drug unit officers in Sligo were aware that Irwin's was not the only gang vying for control of the market.

In the other corner, albeit the underdog, Barry Young had formed his own sub-group in the town. Younger than Irwin and seemingly more mild-mannered, he had no criminal pedigree and often seemed out of place in the underworld of crime, but he was nonetheless lacking nothing when it came to ambition. By 2006 officers were targeting both groups and that year

Irwin was discovered with €67,000 worth of cocaine in County Roscommon, while Young was caught in a graveyard during a dramatic operation when he and an associate, Ian Morrison, then 25, arrived to collect a hidden stash of cannabis. Young admitted his involvement under questioning and accepted full responsibility for the drugs, landing himself a six-year sentence. His co-accused exercised his right to silence and got a heftier ten-year term for the offences. At that time, Young told the court that he was a father of one, had an expensive drug habit and was in fear of a dealer to whom he owed money. Irwin's case dragged on as he delayed entering a plea and sought a judicial review. It wasn't until 2011 that he was sentenced to seven years in prison on the cocaine rap, at which point Young had served his sentence and was back out on the streets free to exert control over the market.

Irwin had wagered badly in many ways. He had underestimated Young and the connections he had made in the prison system, and he'd also allowed him to benefit from timing. While he was in jail one of his own crew, who was a cousin of Young's, was left at a loose end and hooked up with Young, giving him access to many of Irwin's old crew. Young's cousin had already forged a close working relationship with a gang from north Dublin formerly headed up by the missing Sean Dunne, who'd disappeared in Alicante at the height of his power. The Dunne grouping had been taken over by associates and was still running smoothly as a trusted supply line from Spain into Ireland. Young's return wasn't without its problems. He was first targeted by the Real IRA, who demanded a cut of the action, and later he came into the radar of another Republican grouping which modelled themselves on an anti-drug campaign group. Young tried to flex his muscles and for the first time realised that he would have to fight fear with fear. Shy and retiring by nature, he developed an extraordinary ability to compartmentalise his business from his ordinary life and while he was known to be ruthless in the instructions he gave to others when it came to handling any debt owed, he came across himself as a mild-mannered family man. Young's ability to network gave him access to all walks of life and around 2014 he managed to employ the services of a female garda from Sligo who was based in Dublin.

Jimell Henry came from a respectable family and both her father and grandfather had been members of the Garda Síochána, but she had a penchant for cocaine and when Young approached her and offered her money to access the Garda's Pulse computer system she agreed. In late 2014 officers in Sligo became concerned that 'confidential information' appeared to be in the hands of Young and his criminal network and the details could only be coming from within the force. A records search was conducted and it showed that Henry routinely accessed the Pulse system. She was stationed in Ballymun in Dublin, but she was searching for personal details about members of the criminal fraternity in Sligo. In one two-week period she made 980 searches on Pulse, with almost three in every four related to Sligo cases which she had nothing to do with and no responsibility for. Surveillance officers uncovered plans for a secret meeting between Henry and Young in an underground car park in Ballisodare, where they witnessed the pair having a chat. Henry was arrested. Two mobile phones were seized from her car and printouts from the Garda Pulse system were found in her boot. A follow-up search of her home uncovered a quantity of drugs and the investigation found she had used a 'gouger' (burner) phone to pass on information over a five-month period. In what was later described as the first case of its kind to come before the courts, Henry was sentenced to three years in prison with the final 18 months suspended. She pleaded guilty to three charges of disclosing information, four counts of disclosing operational details and two of forging prescriptions. She told the court that she had anxiety issues relating to her mother's death when she was 15 and had taken sanctuary by using cocaine and headshop drugs.

At the same time as corrupting the garda, Young employed Mark 'The Guinea Pig' Desmond to act as an enforcer for him in the Sligo area and paid him enough to convince the violent killer to move to the town from his base in Ballyfermot in Dublin. For Desmond to agree to work full time for Young in such a capacity at that time was for officers a measure of how much control and power Young had accumulated in such a short space of time. Since the double murder of Darren Carey, 20, and Patrick Murray, 19, whose bodies had been found in the Grand Canal in Kildare in the early new year of 2000, Desmond had built a strong reputation. While he was originally charged with the murders, he was never convicted and he had gone on to sow fear wherever he went with his brutal modus operandi of raping young dealers and those who owed him money. He was heavy-set and cut a terrifying figure.

Young had also forged ties with John Gilligan and his network on the Costa Blanca and he met with the crime lord after his release from prison for drug offences following the murder of Veronica Guerin. Gilligan had faced an uneasy return to the criminal underworld after he walked free from Portlaoise Prison in 2013 full of bravado. Within months, in March 2014, he was lucky to survive after being shot up to six times in a house in Clondalkin in a hit carried out by Kinahan killers and sanctioned by the mighty Spanish-based mob. Gilligan had checked himself out of hospital looking old and vulnerable in a wheelchair and disappeared off the scene, but in reality he had employed the services of the Dundon mob to protect him. Inside prison the brothers had worked as bodyguards for under-threat inmates while offering a network of halting sites around the UK where those in fear of their lives could be housed and protected – for a fee. For up to a year Gilligan had used the savings he'd squirreled away in Spain to pay for the protection and had built a close relationship with Ger Dundon along the way. Somehow Gilligan managed to broker a peace deal with the Kinahan mob out of the dispute, which was largely centred on personal differences he had had in prison with one of their lieutenants. Out of immediate danger, he moved to Alicante, where he controlled a number of assets, including the Judges Chamber pub, and villas around the Alicante region. He also had remaining contacts there, including 'Fat' Tony Armstrong, suspected of being behind the disappearance of the violent Westies Stephen Sugg and Bernard Coates in 2003. Slowly Gilligan got back to business, with old contacts and associates still providing him with kudos in the criminal underworld and his age and reputation giving him even more.

Young had prowess along with a willingness to use violence as a means of controlling his corner of the drugs market. He was soon smuggling drugs into the country in modified plant machinery. This sophisticated business model was used by some of the better-known kingpins, like Thomas 'Bomber' Kavanagh, the UK boss of the Kinahan mob, and earlier by Curtis 'Cocky' Warren, the Liverpudlian cocaine lord who had made an appearance in the *Sunday Times* Rich List in 1998 with an estimated £40 million fortune. The tried and tested method of transport worked for Young, and while he made a lot of money, he didn't flash it about – he was all too aware that his earlier engagement with the law meant he remained under the close watch of local and national drug units. He did, however, invest his profits in Spain, working hard to feather a nest for the future in a dream that he would retire under the sun on the Costa Blanca and leave Sligo and his bad deeds behind him.

As Young's enterprise thrived he began to move between Spain and Sligo and set up companies in Dublin and in Alicante. But as his business grew, so too did the Garda response and in January 2019 officers burst into a hotel room in Sligo where Young had been staying with a female associate. The detectives had a search warrant, culminating from a massive investigation into four major drug gangs operating out of the north-west, which had identified Young as the biggest and most influential player of all. The officers rifled through the room, upturning the bed, wardrobe drawers and Young's overnight bag containing clean underpants and socks. Young was polite and shy as usual, as he always was in any dealings with police. He kept his eyes to the floor and failed to make eye contact with the officer who read him his rights and asked him if he wanted to get dressed. The search yielded little in terms of the tools of organised crime, but officers did get what they went for – Young's mobile phone. Despite being at the very top of his game Young had done a lot of his business on the WhatsApp network, but he had been sloppy and had failed to delete or clear the messages. The Gardaí were able to recover texts which included his directions to enforcers to put pressure on debtors to pay up. The phone uncovered how Young was at the very top of a drug-dealing network using 'celebrity' enforcers to collect money and controlling a network of cells, from Donegal to Belfast, supplied by his international contacts. The phone contained a string of messages apparently ordering a hit, instructing 'pressure' to be put on unknown targets to pay up, and warnings that a 'gang of Dubs' would place a 'dirty harry' to their heads and 'let two off' if they didn't. The raid on the hotel room was a game-changer for gardaí in the north-west. Intelligence gleaned from it provided enough justification to deploy a full-time team on organised crime gangs for the next two years under the title Operation Bulldog. Arrests and seizures increased and pressure mounted on Young's criminal network, as well as the man himself, whose number was saved in several phones as 'Boss'.

As part of the strategy, cases focused on offences detailed in the overarching gangland legislation that had been brought in in 2009 but had been a slow burn. This legislation had introduced new offences such as directing a criminal organisation, a problematic thing to prove because of the fluidity of many OCGs – though gradually the Gardaí started to define and name criminal groups and by extension to identify members. The first two men to be jailed under the 2009 legislation were Galway brothers Michael and Edward O'Loughlin, who were originally charged with directing a criminal organisation but pleaded guilty to lesser charges of membership after a decision not to prosecute them on the more serious offences was entered. Both were sentenced to nine years by Judge Martin Nolan at Dublin Circuit Criminal Court in 2012, but both successfully appealed their sentences and reduced terms of six and a half years were imposed on them. As Nolan was the first judge asked to pass sentence under the Act, the Court of Appeal recognised that he had no guidelines on how to approach the sentence. The legislation wasn't used again until 2016, when gardaí policing the Kinahan–Hutch feud began to use it in earnest to target gang bosses, lieutenants, members and associates of the identified mobs. By 2021 the legislation was one of the main tools in the Garda's armament against criminals and in the year to May 2022, 112 arrests were made compared to 72 the previous year and just 24 up to June 2019. Of the 112, eight were for directing and 86 for participation. In September 2021 senior Kinahan mobster Peadar Keating pleaded guilty to directing a feud murder plot and was handed down 11 years.

Buoyed by these successes, gardaí in Sligo focused on Young and the possibility of bringing him before the courts as the first regional kingpin for directing a criminal organisation, a charge carrying a maximum sentence of life imprisonment. As pressure from gardaí mounted on Young and his activities, seizures and arrests followed and with them came the unwanted attention that put pressure on his carefully balanced business. Over the course of the investigation over €628,000 worth of drugs linked to him were confiscated. The losses created problems for Young in particular as he racked up a debt estimated at €300,000 in a debt owed to Mr Big. Throughout Covid, Young decamped to Alicante where he lived in the sun and used his phone to direct his teams in Ireland. In January 2022 he returned to Ireland for a brief visit but as he tried to return to Spain he was arrested at Dublin Airport. He told gardaí that he had been planning to move to Spain for good.

The following May he pleaded guilty to directing a gang in drug dealing, intimidation and money laundering. The Special Criminal Court heard that he was in a downward cycle of debt with drug suppliers, which had affected his mental health. He had thanked gardaí when he was arrested as he was 'under enormous pressure to pay' those he owed in the final years of his career. During the proceedings Detective Garda Inspector Ray Mulderrig told Fiona Murphy SC, for the State, that thousands of messages, images and videos relating to his criminal activities when he was running the Sligo-based gang had been discovered on Young's phones. Young had 81 previous convictions, he said, and had been sentenced twice for drug dealing. The barrister told the court that at least twenty members operated under Young in a 'hierarchical' command structure and in sub-cells. Five phones associated with Young had led to the arrest of 16 people, six of whom had been placed before the courts on charges of organised crime and money laundering. DI Mulderrig said two kilos of cannabis from a UK associate had been seized in October 2019, leading Young to embark on a path of 'panic, fear, agitation and anger'. Another associate caught with €100,000 worth of cannabis had a number in his phone attributed to Young and saved under 'Boss', while a third associate caught with €328,000 worth of cannabis was indebted himself and was used as a courier by the group.

Michael Bowman SC, for Barry Young, said he'd been under 'enormous pressure' to pay off his own debts and had been looking for 'a way out of the life he made for himself'. There had been a legitimate threat to his life, Bowman said, which had affected his mental health, and he had even 'sought to take his own life'. Mr Bowman said Young described his arrest at Dublin Airport as a 'happy day'. At sentencing he was described as a 'scourge' of his own community and jailed for 11 years on a guilty plea. Justice Tony Hunt said that the Young gang was answerable to more serious outfits. Outside the court Chief Superintendent Aidan Glacken, who had led the operation against Young, said:

> Barry Young has been involved in the sale and distribution of controlled drugs for the last twenty years. He directed and controlled a very large organised crime gang involved in an illegal business in the north-west of the country and this gang had substantial international links. In the pursuit of greed and in the pursuit of money, this organised crime gang has caused much harm, much stress, much destruction to society and families through their reckless nature. Many of those families have suffered from violence, threats and intimidation, which

is unacceptable in today's society. Over the past number of years in Sligo, we have committed very substantial resources to tackle this crime gang and other gangs involved in the drugs business. We will continue this work to dismantle these gangs, including seizing their assets, their cash, whether it be here or abroad.

CHAPTER THIRTEEN

Untangling the Web

Days after Barry Young was led away to prison a story published in the *Irish Independent* by its well-informed crime correspondent Ken Foy stated that the PSNI were considering extraditing him in connection with the murder of the criminal Robbie Lawlor, once he finished his sentence for directing a drugs gang. Of course an extradition could only occur if a charge was levelled by the North's Public Prosecution Service – an individual cannot be transferred just for questioning. The basis of the case would be that he was forced to enlist his own criminal associates in the North to have Lawlor murdered on behalf of the Mr Big drugs mob to help clear his debt. In court, Young's barrister, Michael Bowman SC, had painted a picture of a tortured soul. Barry Young, it was claimed, was a victim of crime himself, having run up a drug debt to a major criminal, who was not named in the court proceedings. He described Young as suicidal and terrified, often staying in bed rather than face another day of slavery to the money he owed to a chain of command above him. Young, he said, had come from a decent, working-class family in Sligo but had developed 'significant drug difficulty' that had led to his debt issues. He'd been looking for a way out, Mr Bowman said, and there was a legitimate threat to his life, which had made him depressed and anxious. In counselling, the barrister said, he'd admitted that he'd sought to 'end it all'.

It was a familiar tale and one that is undoubtedly played out across all levels of organised crime, where money is the fuel of a ferocious and violent underworld economy. Debts are moveable feasts and can change and grow at incredible and irrational levels and mob bosses use fear to call them in. A criminal like Mr Big has shown in the past that he is prepared to kill when it comes to his business and he has been a feared figure for two decades, gaining huge notoriety from the murder of the feared Real IRA boss Alan Ryan. His move on Ryan was a courageous one as it risked a reaction from armed and dangerous paramilitaries from the North, groups that for a long time held sway among the criminal fraternity. While the narrative about Mr Big is a perfectly plausible one it is important to look at the character who was presenting it and the circumstances in which he bared his soul.

Young had proved himself to be clever before the courts in the past, pleading guilty to minimise a jail term he was facing and also previously placing the blame for his drug activities on fear and a debt he claimed he owed someone higher up the chain. He is, of course, entitled to a defence and it is his barrister's job to put that to the court and to represent his client as best he can. However, it also shows a pattern in his dealings with the courts, namely a guilty plea and a depiction of himself as a victim. At his most recent sentence hearing, when he pleaded guilty to directing the activities of a twenty-strong criminal gang, he also claimed that he had no trappings of wealth, that he lived in an ordinary house and that he didn't flash the usual assets of drug dealing that his contemporaries did. He was an ordinary family man, he suggested, and he claimed social welfare payments. But details of the criminal operation he ran and his lifestyle told a different story. The court heard that drug seizures linked to his gang totalled over €628,000 and Young himself had €40,000, in four accounts, at his disposal. His phone contained thousands of local, national and international interactions relating to the sale and supply of drugs through a group of at least twenty people who operated in a 'controlled, hierarchical command structure' of sub-cells who all answered to him. Two associates of Young had been caught with cannabis with a value of €485,000 combined and with cash of €18,000. After his arrest in Dublin Airport, searches uncovered another €36,360 in cash and €145,250 worth of cannabis, €11,000 worth of cocaine and €4,500 worth of Valium and unlabelled diazepam. A search of his home led gardaí to bank and vehicle documents and business papers for a car recovery business called BY Recovery. No yard for the business existed. In early 2019 the investigations had found that money moved through Young's business account to a Spanish one and transfers totalling €35,000 were made ahead of his planned departure for Spain. The money and details of the cash and drugs were just a snapshot of what had been a career of twenty years at the top of the drugs business.

In the months after Young was jailed a team of gardaí travelled to Alicante in Spain and searched five properties they suspected were linked to him. Local gardaí from the Sligo/Leitrim Division as well as officers from CAB and the Drugs and Organised Crime Bureau had worked with Spanish national police to identify and search the properties in the Costa Blanca area. Alicante had long been the seat of power of the criminal John Gilligan, a place he had returned to 16 years after he was jailed for drug offences and acquitted of the murder of Veronica Guerin. In all the time he was in prison Gilligan had fought a lengthy battle with CAB and had managed to hold them back from seizing his Jessbrook home where his wife Geraldine lived for almost two decades between stints in Alicante. That battle was a learning curve for CAB and the issuing of free legal aid to Gilligan at the beginning of the case would inform part of the agency's tactics in the future. In the years afterwards the Bureau had strongly fought applications for free legal aid and appealed decisions made by the High Court in favour of their targets. While they ultimately won the case against Gilligan and his assets held in Ireland the Bureau had long believed that the criminal had stashed money in Spain. By 2004 CAB, then under Chief Bureau Officer Felix McKenna, had identified that he owned the Judges Chamber pub in Alicante and, they believed, up to 15 properties, including luxury villas. At that point Gilligan's sidekick Liam Judge, who officers suspected bought the pub and lands on behalf of his boss, had died of a heart attack. Judge had been in a relationship with Tracey Gilligan, the daughter of Factory John, who went on to own and run the pub for years, along with her mother Geraldine. By 2008 senior

CAB officers met with their Spanish counterparts in an effort to identify the retirement treasure trove. At that point, assisted by the Garda Bureau of Fraud Investigation, the CAB were focused on the pub, five warehouses, two boats, six houses, two motor vehicles and a construction firm. Although none of the assets was in his name the Bureau hoped they could prove illegal cash was used by the gangster to fund the various operations. Despite their efforts the Bureau couldn't get the assets probe over the line with Spanish authorities. McKenna would later admit that Gilligan was not seen as a big enough fish at the time in Spain, a melting pot of major-league criminals from all over the world. It would also take another decade for European police forces to start working together effectively under the Europol banner. While Europe's borders had come down, different work practices, legal systems and general mistrust when it came to sharing intelligence meant that policing took some time to put into practice the hopes of political leaders.

Undoubtedly Gilligan emerged from jail as a washed-up relic in the underworld, a man who'd had it all but was unlikely to muscle back into a new gangland ruled by younger men. But while observers knew that, it still took a hail of bullets to make him see the wood for the trees. He had smugly left Portlaoise Prison in October 2013 and immediately tried to get back into the drugs trade but in March 2014 he was shot numerous times at his brother's home in Lucan. Gilligan survived, but a bodyguard he had hired to protect him, McCarthy–Dundon gang member Stephen 'Dougie' Moran, was shot dead two weeks later. After his release from hospital Gilligan went under the protection of Ger Dundon and moved to the UK where he was moved around a number of halting sites while he recovered from his injuries and tried to negotiate with the Kinahan network to have the threat against him lifted. He returned to Ireland in the intervening years to continue his battle with the CAB but eventually returned to Alicante where in October 2020 he was arrested after Spanish cops uncovered how he was running a new drugs operation and sending pills and hash through the postal service to Ireland and the UK. Gilligan's arrest under Operation Godfather was a hugely publicised affair but he vowed to beat the charges. Months later he was handed a fine and a suspended prison sentence by a Costa Blanca judge after admitting to smuggling cannabis and sleeping pills and being the owner of a weapon found hidden in the back garden of his Spanish home. He'd spent just two months in prison.

The case proved one thing – that Gilligan knew how to work the Spanish system. And he had managed to hold on to any assets that he had accumulated there. For someone like Barry Young, an older criminal like Gilligan can serve as a useful mentor and adviser, and the two had often been seen together. Garda intelligence suggested that Young was very close to the older criminal and was working with him, but at the very least he was attempting to feather his own nest on the Costa Blanca, in the same way Gilligan had, until he was stopped in his tracks at Dublin Airport. The assets recovery investigation is ongoing. So did Young get in way over his head and was he simply operating as a lackey for Mr Big? Or was he a careful and considered mob boss who was running a sophisticated money-laundering and drugs business? If assets are identified and linked to him in Spain it is implausible to suggest that he couldn't have used them to pay off a debt owed, especially if, as he claimed, his life was under active threat and he was suicidal and riddled with anxiety as a result. Young did meet with the suspect Adrian Holland in advance of the killing of Robbie Lawlor, a liaison that the PSNI have told the courts in Northern Ireland was to plan that murder. He has remained adamant that he had nothing to do with the murder and is simply implicated because of a business or personal relationship with Holland. But if Young is proved to have been involved in planning Lawlor's murder he is just one of a cast of many who have come together in the demise of a ruthless killer, a man who lived by the gun and died by the gun.

Whatever the outcome, the story of Lawlor's end, in a postage stamp garden in the heart of republican Ardoyne, is an intriguing window into a world of blood and betrayal that is spun like a spider's web. It brings together a cast of characters whose rise to power tells the story of a changing Ireland, a new order that has replaced terrorism and gathered at phenomenal pace alongside Ireland's wealth and prosperity. Each piece of the jigsaw emerges from a series of sliding doors moments in a violent underworld where murders and feuds shift the balance of power in a dark, ruthless world.

Lawlor was shot dead in Belfast in April 2020, less than three months after coming under suspicion for the murder of Drogheda teenager Keane Mulready-Woods. He was the chief suspect for a spate of gang murders even before he became heavily embroiled in the Drogheda feud, a gang war inflamed after his release from jail in December 2019, intent on getting even for the assassination of his brother-in-law Richie Carberry, a murder he had blamed on Mr Big in a prison phone call shortly after.

Among the gun murders Lawlor was suspected of was that of Kenneth Finn, the right-hand man and best pal of Mr Big, in Coolock in February 2018. Was that murder the primary motive for the Belfast ambush and is it at the heart of the PSNI investigation into at least twenty people they believe came together to carry it out? Just like barrister Joe Brolly's comment in court, it is a 'very, very, very good theory', but it doesn't explain the PSNI's position on the activities of members of the McCarthy–Dundon group. The PSNI remain adamant that they were correct to release Ger Dundon and Quincy Bramble and to unconditionally release Levi Killeen after arresting them in the hours after the assassination. Through the State's counsel they have said that they did initially suspect them but that evidence 'points away' from them having any involvement, that they were innocent players in the grotesque murder and that Ger Dundon's car was hit with a bullet, forcing him to flee Ardoyne as his friend lay dead. The theory suggests that Mr Big, considered a devious criminal, used the Dundon grouping as a smokescreen to try to steer the investigation away from what really happened. But if that is the case, how could he do that without their knowledge and without putting them on a payroll? If they were a smokescreen they were surely part of the plot to kill and therefore criminally involved in the murder. One way or another none of it fits too easily with what happened in the aftermath, which cemented links between the Dundon grouping and Cornelius Price, a close association unknown at the time of the Lawlor murder. Ger Dundon had begun working as Lawlor's bodyguard behind bars after he'd been injured in a shiv attack following the 'Judas' handshake from Price, indicating that the Dublin gangster had no idea the two men were connected.

At that point Price was strongly aligned with Owen Maguire and the pair had fought for control over Drogheda against their one-time underlings, who had been facilitated with guns, weapons and advice from Richie Carberry, Lawlor's brother-in-law and only real boss. During the feud Maguire had been targeted and remains the character with probably the most personal grievance against Lawlor. After all, Lawlor had shot him repeatedly, leaving him paralysed and confined to a wheelchair for the rest of his life. Both Price and Maguire openly celebrated Lawlor's death and on the night of the murder Price had recorded a video, which he released on social media, toasting the demise of his enemy with a glass of Captain Morgan rum. He'd said: 'This is to Robbie Lawlor . . . Rest in Peace . . . Fair play to you, Lee.' Dundon, Bramble and Killeen were in custody in Belfast suspected of murder at the time, but were then released; and later Warren Crossan was quizzed about his role in the killing. But just months later Crossan was dead and Dundon, Bramble and Price were arrested together for taking part in what a court would hear was a complex kidnap plot linked to a debt owed to the Belfast criminal. The plot, which was foiled by police, placed Darren McClean, aka Ger Dundon, and his sidekick Quincy Bramble squarely in the Cornelius Price camp; and while the case against Bramble was not proved, Dundon would end up in jail. The connections would raise the bar for Senior Counsel Joe Brolly and solicitor Ciaran

Shiel's 'very, very, very good theory' around their alleged involvement in the Lawlor murder. Of course, that happened long after women linked to the Dundon gang were caught collecting cash which was handed to them by a senior member of the Maguire grouping in a car park at a midlands filling station a few days after the murder. When they were in custody, gardaí had directly asked Ciara Lynch and her pal Kathleen O'Brien if the money was payment for the Robbie Lawlor murder.

What remains the biggest elephant in the room when it comes to the mystery around the Lawlor murder is the timeline of his death, which occurred days into the biggest encrypted phone hack in the history of policing. At the exact time that killers were circling Lawlor as he made his way to Ardoyne in Belfast, French and Dutch police were live on the phone network of criminals who had no idea that their EncroChat devices had been compromised. No evidence has yet been placed before the courts to suggest that the secrets lie in that hack, but both the PSNI and An Garda Síochána had full access to the communications of criminals at that time. Evidence to the courts in Ireland against Lynch and O'Reilly for money laundering indicated that intelligence provided officers with their exact dealings with the Maguire gang and the planned handover of a sum of €50,000. The operation was run by Garda surveillance units operating under the remit of the Crime and Security Division, where all the EncroChat information was flooding in. The speedy release of the Dundon trio could only be explained by conversations observed on that network and would have to point to a double-cross by the Dundons and Cornelius Price, in an effort to claim the kill and strong-arm money in payment from the Maguires. Undoubtedly both the Dundons and Price would be capable of such an unholy alliance and betrayal. Opportunism is what keeps many in the game.

The murder of Robbie Lawlor was not unexpected; in fact, he was a walking target in the run-up to his death and former Chief Superintendent Mangan believed he was killed because he was not careful enough in the way he was conducting his business. He was using social media, openly operating in Belfast and conducting a clandestine relationship which was under surveillance by his rivals. It is not uncommon for a chaotic character like Robbie Lawlor, who has himself murdered and made enemies, to die in a hail of bullets. Many before him, living in a state of paranoia and making increasingly dangerous decisions, have died in similar fashion, sometimes taken out by a grouping of criminals who feel that they are bad for business. Each killing has a ripple effect and provides opportunities for many, showing how everything that happens has a knock-on effect. For example, after the murders of drug dealers Paul Reay and Roy Coddington on the orders of mob boss Martin 'Marlo' Hyland, there was an open playing field for Price and Maguire to form an alliance and move in on turf stretching south towards north Dublin and north along the eastern seaboard. When Marlo's successor, Eamon 'The Don' Dunne, became too unpredictable he was taken out by the Kinahan organisation because he was deemed bad for their business partners in Ireland.

Ireland's underworld is small and poses risks for those involved in feuding in particular, as it is hard to know who to trust and who has connections with whom. Just as it became apparent after Lawlor's murder that Cornelius Price and Ger Dundon had an association, gangland figures under threat can often find that they are fraternising with the enemy. Feuds like those of the cocaine wars in Dublin and Limerick and later the Kinahan–Hutch feud, which played out over two years from 2016, were difficult to police as sworn enemies often knew everything about one another; from habits to girlfriends to details of family gatherings. Feuding sucks up a huge amount of Garda resources and often suits more business-minded mobsters who are happy to allow the young and volatile to take up the time and energies of the Gardaí while they get on with making money.

Unlike the death scenes of those who'd gone before him – in their beds, on a bar stool or on a street corner – there was nothing familiar about the place where Lawlor fell. That Ardoyne and indeed Belfast was once a no-go zone for Dublin drug dealers is true, but his murder proved that everything had changed. Northern Ireland had long cast a shadow over the criminal underworld in the South through heavily armed terrorist groupings, like the Provisional IRA, that disliked drug dealing and saw themselves as having a role to protect their communities. However, following the ceasefire and the Good Friday Agreement in 1998 came a series of dissident groupings who had made the same claims but who were secretly taxing and often working with drug mobs, just like Alan Ryan's Real IRA. But the murder of Lawlor and his presence in Belfast where he'd been drug-debt collecting proved that there was no longer a border when it came to organised crime and that as long as there was money and business to do there was no political divide.

The story of gangland began to emerge from the first heroin epidemic of the 1980s, which affected the sprawling estates that were built as beacons of hope for impoverished communities saved from crumbling tenements. But with the arrival of drugs, generations of kids grew up in massive open-air drug supermarkets, abandoned by politicians and forgotten by progress. Many, who went on to become the dealers, enforcers and mobs of the future, came from homes where parents were in addiction and where they were failed by the health systems, where they fell through the cracks of education and were soon snapped up by gangs hungry for young blood. Others were born into a life of crime; an often familial and hierarchically structured one with strong pressures to take part. Some chose the life, drawn to fast riches and the lure of danger, inspired by heroes like George 'The Penguin' Mitchell and Christy 'Dapper Don' Kinahan, who flooded the country with drugs and weapons and who got filthy rich over decades. They sit at the very top of a ferocious and violent underworld economy fuelled by a recreational drug market that emerged from Ireland's prosperity. Gone are the Concerned Parents Against Drugs, brave community activists who once stood up to the dealers and ran them out of their neighbourhoods. Weary and beaten down, infected by the IRA and forgotten by politicians, those who marched with placards painted with slogans like 'Drug Dealers Out' are a movement of the past, confined now to grainy archive footage and history books. That growth came with a similar trajectory when it came to murder.

By the mid-1990s, as Dr Enda Dooley recognised in his report *Homicide in Ireland*: 'To a degree the category of organised crime-related homicides has replaced those related to terrorist or subversive motive. Both motive types show similarities. The events are usually planned in advance, involve firearms and are undertaken with direct and indirect assistance.' It was at that time that John Gilligan's gang murdered Veronica Guerin, a moment seen as the crossing of the line and a time when organised crime would be tackled like never before. But in reality his downfall simply left a vacuum for his young protégés to step into his shoes when they should still have been in school. Gilligan had groomed the new generation of dealers, teaching them to be hungry and ruthless, to take what they could and to give two fingers to the State and all its institutions. The feuds that followed in Dublin and Limerick, just as the cocaine boom began, opened up job opportunities for killers like never before, hitmen who could take a gun and end a life for money, then move on to the next job.

The EncroChat phone hack, which went live just days before Robbie Lawlor's death, has probably been the clearest window into the workings of the underworld that law enforcement has ever had. Over an almost three-month period officers had a front-row seat at the telephone exchange of gangland's most prolific, who were ordering drugs, weapons and even murders as casually as ringing a local takeaway while sharing pictures of their pets, their cars and even their feet. Hundreds of kingpins, corrupt police officers and seemingly ordinary business people have been caught up in the huge dragnet that followed, their lifestyles and business dealings played out in a way never seen before and in what they believed was a totally bulletproof method of communication. By the time the EncroChat platform messaged users urging them to get rid of their handsets after realising it had been compromised by law enforcement it was June 2020 and Lawlor had been laid to rest near the grave of his brother-in-law Richie Carberry at Laytown Cemetery. More than 115 million criminal conversations had at that point been intercepted through the hacking of over 60,000 users – chats about blood and betrayal.

Acknowledgements

To all those from our world, and of the underworld, who have given their time and consideration to the events that make up this book.

Thanks to Deirdre Nolan and all at Bonnier books for their continued support and encouragement and for dragging these stories out of me.